PERFECT NEGOTIATION

OTHER TITLES IN THE SERIES

PERFECT NEGOTIATION

All you need to get it right first time

Gavin Kennedy

RANDOM HOUSE

BUSINESS BOOKS

This edition published in the United Kingdom in 2003
by Random House Business Books

3 5 7 9 10 8 6 4

First published in 1992 by Century Business
Random House, 20 Vauxhall Bridge Road, London SW1V 2SA

Random House Australia (Pty) Limited
20 Alfred Street, Milsons Point
Sydney, New South Wales 2061, Australia

Random House New Zealand Limited
18 Poland Road, Glenfield
Auckland 10, New Zealand

Random House South Africa (Pty) Limited
Endulini, 5a Jubilee Road, Parktown 2193, South Africa

Random House UK Limited Reg. No. 954009

Papers used by Random House UK Limited are natural, recyclable
products made from wood grown in sustainable forests. The
manufacturing processes conform to the environmental regulations
of the country of origin.

ISBN 1 8441 3149 1

Companies, institutions and other organizations wishing to make
bulk purchases of any business books published by Random House
should contact their local bookstore or Random House direct:
Special Sales Director
Random House, 20 Vauxhall Bridge Road, London SW1V 2SA

Tel: 020 7840 8470 Fax: 020 7828 6681

www.randomhouse.co.uk
businessbooks@randomhouse.co.uk

Typeset in Sabon by SX Composing DTP, Rayleigh, Essex
Printed and bound in Great Britain by
Bookmarque, Croydon, Surrey

For
John

Contents

In memory of John Blair Benson
(1946–2000)

Preface To The Second Edition

Perfect Negotiation summarizes the approach to negotiation with which I have been closely associated for over thirty years. The contents appear largely as they are presented in The NEGOTIATE Workshop, which features the Four Phases of Preparation, Debate, Propose and Bargain. Indeed the workshop materials, particularly The Negotiators Notebook, have been extensively used to compile this summary, as has my best-selling book, *Everything is Negotiable* (3rd edition, 1997).

Among my colleagues, the late John Benson (formerly Chairman of Negotiate Ltd), contributed the most to the concepts and practice outlined in *Perfect Negotiation*. His typically open and unselfish creativity was apparent throughout all the years of our collaboration since we first undertook the task of training negotiators in 1972. I am sure none of my other colleagues and collaborators will demur if I select him for special mention and state that this book is for him. Nobody in their negotiating approach and skills (both strategic and tactical) got closer than John in their practical work to the principles outlined in *Perfect Negotiation*.

John was adamant that negotiators learned their

trade best by practicing it and our training workshops always have had a practical bias.

In this second edition of *Perfect Negotiation* I have added in some of the chapters, 24 '**Activities**' for readers to undertake as they work through the book. These Activities link the negotiating concepts as they are introduced to your personal experiences, and they are a useful means by which you can recognise their practical relevance, and hopefully, reinforce your understanding. You are advised to stop and carry out the mental exercise arising from each Activity and, perhaps, return to them as you practise the related skills in your daily negotiating.

I have also clarified some ideas in respect of negotiation behaviours, particularly how 'Purple' conditional bargaining may best be understood.

Readers interested in discovering for themselves how we put the principles of *Perfect Negotiation* to work in our training and consulting work should visit Negotiates's web site: www.negotiate.co.uk, or email me: gavin@negweb.com. I am also interested your views on *Perfect Negotiation*.

EX BONA FIDE NEGOTIARI
'Negotiate from good faith'
Gavin Kennedy   Edinburgh 2003

Introduction

There are several approaches to improving our negotiating skills.

Some people advocate 'sink or swim' strategies by sending untrained negotiators to jump in at the deep end. While this approach can sort out the 'doers' from the 'viewers', it is also a hit and miss use of talent and opportunity.

You can also read about how experts have negotiated mega deals in recent corporate history and send for some relevant tips for your own deals. If what you read about is not relevant, you are no further forward.

Likewise, you can listen to the 'streetwise' on how to win through intimidation, bluffs and tactical manipulation. Numerous (mainly American) texts extol the manipulation approach but all suffer from three weaknesses: you forget the appropriate ploy; you select the wrong ploy; your situation was not covered in the text. And even where none of these weaknesses apply there is another problem with manipulation – it alienates those with whom you want to do business.

Some other approaches provide extremely useful insights into negotiation practice, but it is not sufficient to rely on their approach. Selecting criteria for a settlement, for example, is helpful in some negotiations but not in others. If the parties cannot agree on the appropriate criteria, because the criteria will determine the nature of the settlement, we are back where we started.

None of these approaches will necessarily lead you to a lasting improvement in your negotiating skills because they do not provide you with an approach that is at once specific enough to guide you in detailed circumstances and general enough to cover every circumstance.

Perfect Negotiation presents the Four Phases of negotiation which apply to all negotiations, irrespective of the people involved, the interests they serve, the culture and personalities of the negotiators, the issues at stake or the place or circumstances.

Distinguishing between the phases that are common to all negotiators, by identifying the skills appropriate to each phase, negotiators, irrespective of their previous level of performance, can improve their performance dramatically in a short period of time.

Of course further practice is required if the improvement in performance is to become lasting rather than transitory. But given that much of what is required to improve our performance is in fact quite simple and straightforward it is not too difficult to find circumstances and contexts where we can practise on a regular basis.

Perfect Negotiation provides you with the basic situations of the negotiating process. It identifies the skills that work and the pitfalls to avoid. Apply its precepts in your daily negotiations at work, at home, in the community and with your colleagues and you will achieve more of what you want in less time and with less stress than, perhaps, you have been used to up to now.

CHAPTER 1

What is negotiation?

INTRODUCTION

All resources are finite. Animals, and some humans, fight for food, mates and territory, using various forms of dominance and display to decide who gets how much of what and when they get it.

Using, or even threatening, violence can only redistribute wealth, it cannot create it.

Through civilization humans have developed the capacity to distribute the basics of food, mates and territory, and today's vast array of products and services, by means other than violence or the threat of violence.

One of the methods we use is called negotiation.

DEFINITIONS

Negotiation is the process by which we pursue the terms for getting what we want from people who want something from us.

It can also be described as 'a process for resolving conflict between two or more parties whereby both or

all modify their demands to achieve a mutually acceptable compromise.'

Negotiation is a synonym for trading; for exchang-
ing things we have that others want, for things we want
from them. Implicit in every negotiation is the statement: 'Give me some of what I want, and I will give you
some of what you want.'

ALTERNATIVES TO NEGOTIATION

Conflict cannot always be resolved by negotiation. There
are alternatives including 'agreeing to disagree' (e.g. a
potential customer deciding not to buy at the price asked).

There are several alternatives to negotiation, all of
them familiar to every adult, and to many children, who
are used to switching between them to get what they want:

Persuasion ('Our services are good value')

Persuasion is often tried first when people want something, but it is seldom successful when their interests
clash. All selling skills are persuasion skills; if you
already have double glazing you are unlikely to be persuaded to buy a new set of windows.

Giving in ('OK, I'll cut prices by 30 per cent')

Giving in is an option when the odds are overwhelming,
or the issue is trivial. It involves giving in to your oppo-
nent's wants, or doing without your own. We give in
every time we visit a supermarket for groceries. We
normally accept the prices on the goods, pay them at the
checkout and take them home. Giving in and negotiation do not go well together. It encourages difficult
negotiators to demand more.

Coercion ('Meet my demands, or else!')

In some circumstances you might coerce people to do what you want, but this risks long-term relationships and provokes hostility and revenge. Coercion in a negotiation context is unwise. It hardens attitudes and leads to damaging counter-blows.

Problem solving ('How can we avoid this problem happening again')

Where all parties recognize that they share a problem, as well as trust each other, it might be possible to use problem-solving techniques.

Instruction ('Take this package to despatch')

Instruction is effective in certain cases. An example is the employer/employees relationship where instructions are accepted by the employee, in specific areas, in return for their wages. They may, however, obey resentfully and await an opportunity to 'get their own back'.

Arbitration ('Which is fairest, my or her proposals?')

Arbitration is an option in cases where agreement cannot be reached. It can, nevertheless, be unpopular because it reduces the negotiator's power and because the parties can renege if they are not legally bound to comply with the agreement reached.

ALL METHODS HAVE A ROLE TO PLAY

- No method of decision making is superior to another in all circumstances
- Each is appropriate in some circumstances but not in others

- When negotiating it is not normally advisable to give in as this tends to encourage further demands
- Likewise, coercion is risky when negotiating, as it can severely damage the relationship between negotiators
- Choose the most suitable method for the circumstances

No method of getting what you want is superior to any of the others

They all have a role to play in some circumstances where they would fail in others. *Perfect Negotiation* is concerned with the techniques of negotiation as a method you can use to get what you want.

WHEN IS IT APPROPRIATE TO NEGOTIATE?

- Not always
- When we are given no choice
- When we need each other's consent
- When it is the only way to get what we want
- When the outcome is uncertain
- When the stakes justify our time and effort

CHAPTER 2

The four phases of negotiation

INTRODUCTION

All negotiations, no matter what the issues, the history, the culture or the context, can be analysed in terms of the four phases of negotiation. These main phases were identified from the analysis of actual industrial relations negotiations from 1972-4. They proved to be a helpful training tool, as well as a useful operational tool, for negotiators in various business, personal and international contexts. Most negotiation skill programmes now use some or other version of the four phases, which is a suitable testimony to their relevance.

WHAT IS 'PERFECT NEGOTIATION'?

The concept of perfect negotiation is a practical framework through which a trainee negotiator can understand, and cultivate, the necessary skills to conduct successful negotiations.

In this way, the negotiation process is divided into the four main phases through which it will progress before an agreement is reached. These phases are differentiated from each other by the different sets of skills relevant to each one.

A negotiator may fail to exploit these phases as a result of inexperience, lack of training or simple lack of practice. When agreement is eventually reached it is unlikely to represent the best deal possible. It is for this reason that the skills associated with the phases are emphasized.

THE FOUR MAIN PHASES OF NEGOTIATION

Prepare – What do you want?

- Decide what you want and prioritize (value) your wants

Debate – What do they want?

- Listen to what they say they want
- Disclose what you want but not the terms on which you might settle
- Ask open questions and listen to answers
- Listen for signals, which indicate a wilingness to consider movement

Propose – What could you trade?

- Use 'if . . . then' language. (If they meet some of your wants, then you might consider meeting some of their wants)
- Keep quiet and wait for a response
- Do not interrupt proposals

Bargain – What will you trade?

- Trade wants to agree to specific solutions
- Always conditional 'if . . . then'
- Record what has been agreed

POINTS TO REMEMBER

- All negotiations have a common structure
- Negotiators are always in one or other of the four phases common to all negotiations
- Identifying the phase you are in helps you to move the negotiations forward

DIVERSIONS AND INTERRUPTIONS

Negotiations are often messy, involve many diversions and interruptions, and do not always move forward in a tidy fashion from preparation to agreement. Fortunately, however, this does not weaken the four phase approach because it was from the real world of negotiating, with all its complexities, that the original anlaysis identified the phases and the sub-steps that link them.

FLEXIBILITY OF THE FOUR PHASES

It is perfectly acceptable to go backwards and forwards between the phases. For example, while some preparation is completed before the first face-to-face meeting, additional preparation might be necessary because of what you discover once you meet the other negotiators. While debate may be a prelude to a proposal, the proposal may lead to more debate – before you get to another proposal! And so it goes on. For example, asking a question about a proposal or a bargain returns you to the debate phase.

We do not necessarily negotiate in a strict order from phase 1 to phase 4. It is possible to start with debate (phase 2) to learn what is wanted and then to adjourn to prepare (phase 1) our response. Some negotiations begin with proposals (phase 3) and then go on to a debate (phase 2). When a question us asked to clarify a bargain (phase 4), we are back in debate (phase 2). During negotiations we might return to preparation (phase 1) several times.

All negotiations involve varying combinations of the four phases. Knowing which phrase you are in enables you to adapt your own behaviour to the circumstances.

For each phase there are certain techniques that work and other techniques that do not.

MANAGE YOUR NEGOTIATION

Once you understand the role of the four phases in negotiation you are able to 'manage' your negotiations.

Instead of relying on nothing more than an instinctive reaction to the other negotiator, you are able to choose how to respond. You know which phase you are in, which actions or reactions on your part will help the phase to move forward and which will hinder progress. You are no longer guessing what to do next in your negotiations because you are able to manage what you are doing.

Whether the other negotiator is aware of the phases or not makes little difference. If they are aware of them, this will assist both of you to move competently towards a settlement, if one is possible. If they are not aware of the phases their reactions may be comparatively disorganized, or badly managed, but yours will not be and this will give you a negotiating edge.

Activity 1

Think about recent negotiations and try to recollect the phases you went through, or during your next negotiation observe the phases. Did you undertake some pre-negotiation preparation? How long proportionately would you say you spent in debate? At what point were proposals offered and by which side? What about specific proposals or bargains that you could agree to accept? How was the outcome recorded?

A proposal is a proposal in any language. Their proposals may be poorly phrased, unconditional or just a one-way demand. Yours will always be conditional. The difference will help to educate them in how to do business: nobody gets what they want unless and until you are offered some of what you want.

They may be stuck in an argument while you prefer to explore each other's wants in a constructive debate. Your understanding of the role of each phase assists your efforts to find a solution. Whether they anxiously work through a phase or stumble through it makes little difference to you. Your approach is a conscious application of effective behaviour in each phase. You – and they – will notice the difference.

CHAPTER 3

Phase one:
how to prepare

INTRODUCTION

Preparation, or lack of it, will become immediately apparent as negotiations get under way. A negotiator who arrives poorly prepared is really only in a position to react to events, rather than lead them. As this lack of preparation becomes apparent, the other negotiator will naturally feel strengthened in their position. They will therefore become more confident and committed to their own demands, particularly if it is not appropriate for you to adjourn to prepare properly.

A negotiator must nevertheless avoid using preparation time to rehearse a dogmatic defence of any given position, however deeply held, or to adopt an aggressive approach to the other negotiator's position. Constructive preparation is vital.

DEFINING YOUR WANTS

You will negotiate to get what you want. In the preparation phase you will decide or confirm what you want. Hence, the question you should ask yourself is: what do

I want to happen as a result of this negotiation? The answer will be a list of your wants.

Merely quantifying what you want is obviously not an automatic guarantee that you are going to get it. In the course of the negotiation you will have to modify your own wants, to a greater or lesser extent, to take account of the competing wants of the other negotiator.

Activity 2
What do you think a mother meant when she comforted her son, disappointed in a relationship: "Son, sometimes we get what we want and sometimes we get what we get"?

It also is worth noting that opening negotiations may involve the re-opening of previously settled issues: in the course of the negotiation for an overall advantage it is possible to lose some items which hitherto may have been taken for granted.

MUTUAL OBJECTIVES

In pursuing your own objectives through negotiation you must, of course, give consideration to the other party's objectives, and their approach in attaining them. Establishing the other party's wants and gauging their priorities can be difficult. Particularly so, as they may think it is in their interests to conceal any such priorities and convince you that their demands are all of equal importance. You cannot baulk at such 'bluffing' ploys, however, if you yourself are inclined to take this approach. The other party's wants are obviously of some importance, but they are only really of significance insofar as they influence the attainment of your own objectives.

Through negotiation you might get what you want on their terms, or they might get what they want on your terms, or both of you might get some of your wants on each other's terms.

WHAT IS THE NEGOTIATION ABOUT?

All negotiations take place in a context which influences the negotiator's behaviours and their aspirations, the types of issues that are addressed and the range of possible outcomes.

WHAT ARE MY INTERESTS?

An interest is whatever motivates you to prefer your solution to a negotiable problem. It is the reason why you prefer this or that solution to the solution offered by the other party.

Employees prefer higher to lower wages because it is in their interest to have a higher standard of living – it gives them more choice. Improving their living standards is an interest, a wage increase is an issue and the amount of the increase they seek is a position.

Interests are the fears hopes and concerns that motivate people to support or oppose policies that affect them.

Activity 3
Think of a policy (minimum order value, pressure on prices, rules about returning goods, quality guarantees, notice of cancellation, and so on) towards suppliers or customers that is pursued by an organisation with which

you are familiar. Can you identify why this policy is pursued? What interests do you think might be driving this policy and whose interests do they serve?

WHAT ISSUES HAVE TO BE ADDRESSED?

An issue is anything over which the negotiators have discretion. For example, issues could include the price of a product, the quantity available, where a country's boundary line runs, how loose or tight a contract clause must be and so on. Through negotiation, issues become the decisions of the parties to the agreement. The negotiable issues are the Agenda items to be negotiated.

WHAT DO YOU WANT?

Wants are preferences in respect of the issues. They are the decisions you prefer to arrive at, though what you want may have to be modified as a result of accommodating the other negotiator's wants. For example: I may want to pay a lower price for your business because of the uncertainty about future profits, while you may want a higher price because you wish to retire in a state of affluence. Through negotiation we might be able to find a way to meet both our wants (e.g. a purchase price in two tranches, one on my acquiring the business, which meets my concerns, the other when its true profits are proven, which meet your ambitions). In other words, by negotiating for our wants we aim to deliver our interests.

List and prioritize wants
For every issue, you should write down what you want.

You can be as vague or specific as you need and for the moment you need not concern yourself with what the other negotiator might want.

Now assess how important each of these wants is to you. In short, prioritize your wants. Some wants will be more important than others, some wants you may not be sure about just yet. You may use any categories of importance that you find convenient, such as high, medium and low (or Crucial, Important and Desirable, or even simply 1, 2 and 3):

- *High importance*: those that you must get if you are to agree at all. These represent the 'bottom line' or 'limit position'; the objectives without which a negotiator is not prepared to reach any agreement
- *Medium importance*: those objectives that you would prefer to attain if you could, but which are not critical
- *Low importance*: those objectives that you would like to attain if you could, but would not let a failure to get them jeopardize the deal

Caution: to categorize an issue as being of 'low importance' does not mean that the issue is of no importance. Any issue that is of more importance to the other negotiator than it is to you is not a valueless 'give away'; it could become a valuable tradable. Such tradable issues of low importance to us may be of greater importance to them, and in negotiation we try to exchange movement in our positions on items of low importance for movement on items of higher importance to us.

Evaluate wants
Next you must assign ranges of possible values to each of the issues you have prioritized. For example, you may

set a quantitative range, such as: '£105 to £150'. You may equally set a qualitative range, such as: 'will deliver by Friday' to 'use best endeavours to deliver by Friday'. This requirement is based on the notion that negotiators do not enter the negotiations exactly where they intend to settle – if they did this would imply that there was no movement possible and the negotiation would degenerate into a battle of wills or a power struggle. Negotiating from fixed and inflexible positions is extremely difficult. Despite being easily avoidable, it remains the most common cause of deadlock between negotiators. Giving yourself a range gives you flexibility as well as a greater chance of reaching an agreement.

ENTRY AND EXIT POSITIONS

Hence, you will tend to enter the negotiation with statements of requirements on the issues which you certainly know, and the other negotiator almost certainly will assume, will not be your final position. They will know that wherever you start from, you are probably willing to move somewhat further. The range therefore will begin with an 'entry' position and end with an 'exit' position. This also provides the rationale for never accepting a negotiator's first offer – because wherever they open there is another position, better for you, where they will go before they close.

Where to enter and where to exit?
Where you enter will depend on the circumstances and on what you believe you can credibly defend to the other negotiator. Unrealistic or overly ambitious objectives should be abandoned prior to the negotiations as putting them forward could antagonize the other nego-

tiator into similarly unrealistic demands. Where you exit will also depend on the circumstances and on what options you have in case you cannot reach agreement.

If you are sure you have many alternative options, your entry point might be relatively ambitious and your exit point relatively close to where you began. If you are not so sure of your strengths, or are convinced that you have few alternative options (few customers, fewer opportunities) you are likely to enter relatively 'softly' and be prepared to exit even more 'softly' if you have to. Nevertheless, it is a common failing for diffident negotiators to err on the side of caution, aiming lower rather than higher (they often negotiate with themselves first!)

RECORD PREPARATION DETAILS

The details of your preparation can be recorded on a single sheet of paper. The detail you wish to go into will depend on the importance of the negotiation. No matter how short your time, however, some consideration of the issues to be decided will automatically improve your negotiation performance:

- What you want from the negotiation
- The relative importance you attach to your wants
- How you would present your wants, in the form of a range from your entry position to your exit position

Effective handling of face-to-face interaction, the debate phase, will do much to consolidate the advantages gained from improved preparation.

HOW TO PREPARE – EXAMPLE

A manufacturer uses a specialized machine tool for some high-quality components. A problem has emerged with the availability of the machine due to some recurring maintenance fault, delays in the supplier's technicians arriving to correct the fault, and errors on the part of the operators.

The manufacturer has arranged a meeting with the supplier to resolve the problems. It is anticipated that the meeting will lead to negotiation. Independent of this situation, the supplier had already approached the manufacturer with a request to increase prices on the grounds that the maintenance contract was unprofitable.

What might the manufacturer's negotiator do in preparation for the meeting? Apart from collecting recent data on the machine's unavailability and the reasons for each incident, the negotiator would begin to assess the question: What do we want?

Negotiation		Relative	Range	
Issues	*Wants*	*Importance*	*Entry*	*Exit*
1. Machine availability	Maximized	High	100%	70%
2. Service delays	Minimized	Medium	3-hour call out	24 hours
3. Operator errors	Minimized	Low	Free training by supplier	Training

CHECKLIST FOR PREPARATION

- What do you want to happen as a result of this nego-
  tiation?
- What are the negotiable issues?
- What do you want for each issue?
- Rank each want by its importance to you
- High – critical – potentially no deal
- Medium – important but not critical
- Low – like to get but not critical for self – may be
  important for other negotiator
- What are your Entry and Exit limits?
- Entry terms should be credible and defensible
- Exit terms are your 'walking away' positions
- All prepared positions are subject to revision if cir-
  cumstances suggest changes are advisable

Common mistakes to avoid
- Not finding time to decide what you want
- Confusing 'let's hear what they have to say' with
  preparation
- Being unrealistic when deciding on your Entry and
  Exit points
- Not prioritizing your wants
- Not setting a range for each want

CHAPTER 4

Phase two:
how to debate

INTRODUCTION

Debate is the most common form of interaction between negotiators. It accounts for an estimated 80 per cent of time spent in negotiation.

This makes debate a key area for self-improvement because by your conduct in debate with other negotiators you can slow down, hinder, deadlock or alternatively promote a settlement. This is because you can control two things during debate; how you present yourself and how you react to the other negotiator (no matter how they are behaving).

Your approach to debate will influence the progress and outcome of the negotiation. This will not just be at a particular stage, either, as the debate phase will continue throughout the negotiation as a whole.

Coping with debate, getting it to work in favour of your negotiating objectives and not against them, will significantly improve your performance as a negotiator.

USING DEBATE TO GAUGE THE OTHER
NEGOTIATOR'S VIEWS

Preparation will have clarified your own standpoint on the issues. You now have to gauge the other negotiator's views. Preparation will also have included conjecture on your part which you will now have the opportunity to test.

The other negotiator will normally need little encouragement to disclose their opinions. They will represent their entry position, and all successive 'current' positions, as their exit position as far as you are concerned.

The more you can find out about their position – by questioning and clarification – the more information you can gain about their commitment to their position and the direction in which they may be prepared to move.

Debate provides a crucial opportunity to glean information about the other negotiator's objectives and attitudes. In this way you can gauge their commitment and identify their interests and intentions; equally important, you will discover their inhibitions. An interest will encourage someone to say 'Yes', an inhibition will encourage them to say 'No'.

In negotiation, inhibitions are more powerful than interests. If somebody expresses inhibitions motivating them to say 'no' to a proposition, it is essential to address these inhibitions rather than try to persuade them to forget them by highlighting the reasons why you think they should say 'yes'.

Negative inhibitions, which are often emotional, become stubborn de-motivators if ignored or disregarded. By changing an inhibition into an interest you will be more likely to be successful in a negotiation.

For example, the price of a new house may be less

important than when you are required to pay the current owner the money. If she requires payment within 30 days and this is not possible given your finances, her 30-day deadline inhibits you saying 'yes' to the deal. If, however, she responds by extending the payment period to three months, and if her extension removes your inhibition, a 'yes' decision becomes an interest to you – so much so, in fact, that you may be prepared (and she should require you) to pay slightly more for the house, which is in her interest too!

Activity 4

In what circumstances lately have you considered *when* you were paid more important than *what* you were paid (or vice versa)?

Interests and inhibitions are important factors in a person's attitudes to what is debated.

Neither factor will be immediately obvious to you, and you will initially be reliant upon assumptions. Debate will therefore give you the opportunity to test these assumptions. Foreknowledge of another party's plans, wants or objectives will also offer you the chance to test their candour or basic honesty.

Effective use of debating time should allow you to explore each other's inhibitions as well as your own. Creating this open dialogue between both parties will probably have one of two consequences. It will either acknowledge the mutual benefits of negotiating a settlement or it will demonstrate that a settlement is neither possible nor desirable.

If you concentrate on the task of debate – to find out what the other negotiator wants and let them know what you want – you will avoid disruptive diversions and destructive argument.

FEATURES OF DESTRUCTIVE ARGUMENT

Destructive argument is a temptation at this phase because it helps prevent too close an examination of opening positions. It is an all-too-common feature of many negotiations, and is most likely to arise where parties are highly committed, anxious, or angry, even. A prime example would be the unhelpful practice of interrupting. A simple, yet fundamental, step that you can take to improve your performance in negotiations is to dispense with the habit of interrupting other people.

Other features of destructive argument, to be avoided, include the following:

- Regularly point-scoring on issues
- Attacking or blaming somebody for a problem
- Sarcasm and other forms of disrespect
- Personal insults
- Ascribing ulterior motives to other people
- Not listening to what others are saying
- Rising to provocation

Consequences of destructive argument

Few people, for example, can resist point-scoring – reminding the other party of their past failures.

The blame and attack/defence cycles are well-established elements of destructive argument. When someone is attacked they will instinctively defend themselves, however irrelevant the attack is to the main objectives of the negotiation. Attempts to apportion blame will either provoke spontaneous resistance or efforts to retaliate by passing the blame back to you.

As an attack/defence cycle proceeds, emotional tension and personal attacks are evident and interpersonal relationships suffer damage as a result.

Negotiators' inhibitions, including their fears and concerns about your intentions, are reinforced by destructive argument. Inhibitions hinder negotiation and can even obstruct an agreement which is mutually advantageous.

To someone wholly concerned with winning, any movement – no matter how minor – is a loss. The result of such behaviour can only be to drive the negotiators apart.

REDUCE TENSION

Negotiations often begin with a degree of tension present. This can be because of the history of the relationship: warring nations, poor industrial relations, failures to perform past or current contracts, squabbling relatives etc. It can also be because the negotiators do not know each other, or are uncertain of what is about to be decided. If tension is present, avoiding it worsening into outright hostility is imperative.

Negotiators can do a lot to reduce tension by what they say and how they speak to each other. You can help yourself to reduce tension if you remember that your sole task in debate is to assess what the other negotiator wants and to inform them of what you want.

Establish rapport

You can begin by establishing rapport with the other negotiator. Rapport establishes your relationship. It sets the tone of the relationship in the first few minutes. Your tone can work against you if you appear hostile (because you feel angry). You can also undermine your negotiating position by too subservient a tone in which you are so desperate to be friendly that you sacrifice your own wants unilaterally.

Therefore:

- Show and earn respect
- Follow culturally-set norms of greeting and non-business talk

Determine the order of business

Next, set an agenda to organize the meeting. This can be done formally in writing or informally with a verbal summary of what you propose to discuss. Always invite amendments and comments on the subjects and their order.

Describe what you are seeking

In describing the broad conclusions you are seeking, reassure the other negotiator(s) by using tactful and non-threatening terms.

For example:

- 'I hope at the end of the meeting we have agreed to a financial package that will secure the company's future'
- 'Difficult as these problems are, I am willing to look at any constructive proposal we can come up with to solve them'
- 'My intention is to see if we can agree heads of terms at this meeting, for more detailed discussions later'

You must explain your entry position before you can expect the other negotiators to move towards it. Each party must know the other's entry position in order to assess its proximity to their own limit.

Avoid threats

Do not state or imply a threat in your opening remarks. For example:

- 'If we cannot reach a sensible settlement here, we may have to consider litigation'

Threats are certain to provoke resentment. Your opposite number does not need to be reminded of the consequences of failure before you start. Threats either produce counter-threats or statements of defiance and are thus likely to lead to argument before negotiations have even begun.

Listen positively

To find out what the other party wants, listen to what they say (the more they talk – and the less you do – at this stage, the better). Ask them questions about what they want, and listen to their answers. Anyone who tells you what they want in negotiation is doing you a favour – so if they launch into a monologue you should listen for clues as to their wants and not feel obliged to interrupt.

You must support positive listening behaviour with positive talking behaviour – making sure you use the time effectively. One way to do this is to ask open questions which encourage explanation and elaboration by the other negotiator.

USE QUESTIONS

Questions are both underrated and badly-used negotiating tools. Below average negotiators do not ask enough, if any, questions and many negotiators who do ask questions ask the wrong kind in the wrong tone.

Keep doors open if you want to be an effective negotiator. Never say 'No', instead ask an open question such as 'What are you offering in return for our acceptance of your suggestion? . . .' Open questions unlock doors.

Don't disagree – always ask them an open question instead. When a negotiator makes a statement that you disagree with, you will achieve little if you tell them they are wrong. While you are explaining why they are wrong, they will be thinking of how to defend themselves, perhaps by raising irrelevant matters, perhaps by attacking you. It is much more effective for you to ask open questions about the basis for the statement that you disagree with and for them either to show their statement to be true (in which case you can change your own position without loss of face), or to show that their own statement is false (in which case they can retract without feeling aggrieved).

Right and wrong questions to ask
Examples of the wrong types of question to ask include:

- 'Are you listening?'
- 'Are you serious?'
- 'Do you think I am stupid?'
- 'Is that your final offer?'

These are tension-inducing questions that are likely to lead you away from an early settlement, perhaps into irretrievable deadlock.

Examples of the right type of questions to ask include:

- 'What criterion are you using?'
- 'What are your priorities?'
- 'How do you calculate those numbers?'
- 'How do you feel about these issues?'

These questions seek information using an open question format which normally requires an extended answer, rather than a simple 'yes' or 'no'. By using words like 'what', 'why', 'when', 'how', 'where', and 'who', you invite the other negotiator to explain themselves and to disclose their wants.

When asking open questions it is essential to make considered use of language. 'How did you arrive at that conclusion?' should elicit useful details about the other negotiator's reasoning. 'Do you think I am stupid?', on the other hand, which you might be equally tempted to say, would provoke a counter-productive emotional defence, telling you nothing.

SUMMARIZING

Before you make any response to a detailed proposal it is a good idea to summarize what they have proposed. You can either ask them to do it, or alternatively go through it yourself, highlighting any implications and their (not your) attitude towards them.

Summarizing is positive behaviour. It has many uses:

- Simplifies complex issues
- Helps re-focus wandering negotiations
- Reassures them that they are being taken seriously
- Gives you time to think

Activity 5
Practise the difficult art of summarizing (especially if you are not paying attention) by summarizing what you have just read of four benefits of this technique.

ARGUMENTS, PRINCIPLES AND OPINIONS
CANNOT BE NEGOTIATED

We can only negotiate proposals and therefore debate is more effective if it informs the negotiators of what each wants, because their proposals will have to address those wants. We cannot negotiate the 'truth' or 'falsity' of someone's beliefs, values, principles or opinions. These lead only to argument.

MANAGEMENT OF MOVEMENT

Parties to a negotiation must move from their current preferred solution to some other acceptable solution if an agreement is to be reached. The negotiator's problem is how to make this happen – how to ensure that movement by one side is reciprocated by movement on the other side.

Negotiation can be seen as the 'management of movement'. We trade movement on our part for movement on theirs, either on the same issue or for movement on other issues. Setting up these mutual traded movements is a key skill in negotiation. For example: 'If you accept a lower price per unit, then we will agree to place orders for a minimum quantity per month.'

The principal motivations for moving are incentives (benefits of agreeing) and sanctions (penalties for not agreeing). These forces may be explicit (attention being drawn to the consequences of agreeing or disagreeing) or implied. There are also disadvantages from agreeing and disadvantages from disagreeing to a proposition and the negotiator has to weigh the balance between them. Crudely if the disadvantages from agreeing are outweighed by the disadvantages from disagreeing, the negotiator is inclined to be more favourable to the proposition (and vice versa).

Negotiation is motivated by self-interest. People negotiate because the other party offers them an incentive or threatens them with a sanction. Without either of these there is no negotiation. If you are satisfied with the *status quo* – have nothing to trade and want nothing on offer – you will not negotiate.

However committed the parties appear to be to their position, and however unwilling to trade, they would not be involved in negotiating if they were not willing to consider moving towards an agreement.

DEADLOCK

Deadlock can occur when both parties rely on the strategy of sticking to their current position until the other is willing to move. If both sides adopt this approach there will be no movement.

Why should a party be unwilling to negotiate? Distrust and tension may be present. One party may see its interests as being best served by resisting change of any kind and maintaining the existing situation. Only if they come to believe that the potential outcome is likely to be an improvement in the existing situation, or less damaging than the possible consequences of the existing situation, will they be willing to move.

Why else is movement avoided?
Because movement can be interpreted as weakness. If you refuse to move for long enough you hope the other party may ultimately 'surrender'; but they may be following the same strategy and hoping you will surrender, in which case the negotiation may fail completely.

Inexperienced negotiators often fall into the trap of giving away too much too soon, resulting in an unsatisfactory agreement, because a generous free gift concession normally does not promote traded reciprocal movement.

Balancing firmness and flexibility

There is a dilemma faced by all negotiators; how do you suggest flexibility in your entry requirements without giving in? Once you move from a position, there is a danger that one move will follow another, until you have nothing left to negotiate and nothing to show for your movement. Below-average negotiators do not move at all. They try intimidation, with the intention of forcing the other negotiator to give in, or in the hope that they will do so. Effective negotiators, however, listen and watch for signals.

LOOKING FOR SIGNALS

Every negotiation has at least two solutions to the same problem – the solution that meets your wants and the solution that meets the other party's wants. Your strategic task is to arrive at an agreed solution, which almost certainly will be different from either of the two solutions with which the negotiation began. Hence, you look for signals, or signs of a willingness to consider movement.

Signalling behaviour provides a method with which to handle movement confidently.

A signal is a means by which parties indicate their willingness to negotiate on something. It is also more than that: it implies a willingness to move only if it is reciprocated by the other side and not treated as a first step on the slippery slope to surrender.

Advantages of signalling behaviour
- Can be used to break the cycle of circular argument
- Allows you to make new proposals without being seen to give in
- Familiar behaviour we often use – nothing new to learn

What are signals?
Signals are qualifications attached to a statement. For example:

- 'Our normal price is . . .'
  (But we have a different price for special circumstances)
- 'It would be extremely difficult . . .'
  (But not necessarily impossible)
- 'We do not want to be locked into this deal . . .'
  (We need an escape clause)

The signal suggests the possibility of agreement if the other party's proposal is amended in some way. It is an invitation to the other party to move. It says that although the present proposal is unacceptable, it could be negotiable if put in another form.

RESPONDING TO SIGNALS

Signals hint at the possibilities of movement if, and only if, the other negotiator responds positively. At this stage the category of response is crucial. Of course, if the other negotiator attacks the signaller you can be sure that they will slip back towards argument:

- 'I don't care about your normal prices'
- 'So after an hour of pretending it was impossible to change the contract, you now agree it can be changed'
- 'You are either in the deal totally or there is no deal at all'

Summarize signals

The most effective way to respond to a signal is to confirm what you heard by summarizing what is said to you – even if you do not yet see how the signal helps you – and then encourage the other party to expand on their tentative hints by asking open questions about the signal. For example:

- 'Under what circumstances would you consider a non-list price?'
- 'How could we make it easier for you to re-examine this clause?'
- 'How can we address your concerns about being locked in?'

This type of open question can reveal their wants in greater detail and what wants of yours they might be prepared to meet.

Signalling does not inevitably lead to agreement, nor resolve conflict. It makes negotiation about the issues possible and leads to the possibility of agreement. Signals lead to proposals – they are the bridge between debate and attempts to trade.

Activity 6

Think of a recent dispute (domestic, work, neighbourhood, etc.,) and try to recall the signals that were employed to secure movement from the entrenched positions. If you cannot recollect any, how did the people move from their initial positions?

ADJOURN

Wherever possible, you should take an adjournment at this point, to consider what you have learned about the other negotiator's wants, and to assess the initial reactions to the statement of your own wants. In short, you should return to the preparation phase to plan your movement to the proposal phase. Taking a short break is not as difficult as it might seem. Very few negotiations over major issues are settled at a single meeting and using a natural break in those that are is not beyond most negotiators to suggest or arrange.

CHECKLIST FOR SIGNALLING

- Are there any signs of potential movement in the debate?
- What signals have you made to indicate your own willingness to consider moving?
- If they have been ignored, how might you reword them?
- What is the cause of the other party's 'stonewalling'? Confidence, or lack of it?
- Test 'stonewalling' by a specific signal linked to a direct call for them to reciprocate
- If there is still no response you can:
  - suspend the negotiation
  - require them to seek authority to revise their position
- Avoid making unilateral concessions in the hope that they will respond because this only rewards their intransigence
- Listen for their use of non-absolute and qualified statements of their position, or references to their inhibitions

- Ask them to elaborate on the implications of them (their best move is to seek your commitment to respond)
- Respond positively, but vaguely. For example: 'I am always prepared to consider constructive suggestions for improving the acceptability of my proposals'

Memory joggers
– ignoring signals prolongs debate
– listen more talk less
– respond and reciprocate positively
– reward signals not intransigence

Common mistakes to avoid
- Ignoring signals
- Moving in response to intransigence
- Not exploring the implications of a signal
- Not reacting positively to a signal

CHECKLIST FOR DEBATE

Avoid the following:

- Mocking
- Interrupting
- Point-scoring
- Attacking
- Blaming
- Talking too much
- Shouting them down
- Sarcasm
- Threatening

Practise the following:

- Listening
- Asking questions for clarification
- Summarizing issues neutrally (and briefly)
- Asking them to justify their case on an item-by-item basis (watch for signals)
- Being non-committal about their explanations
- Looking for clues about their priorities and testing their commitment to their positions
- Seeking and giving information

Common mistakes to avoid
- Only asking closed questions
- Not listening
- Arguing to 'win'
- Not summarizing
- Making mountains out of molehills

CHAPTER 5

Phase three: how to propose

INTRODUCTION

You will be ready to propose when you are able to summarize what the other negotiator wants and when you have informed the other negotiator of what you want. In your preparation you identified the issues and what you wanted. Now you must think about what the other negotiator wants, and, if possible their order of priorities.

WANTS

Competing wants

In stating their wants, they are likely to have revealed their entry positions. This gives you crucial information. By comparing their wants with yours and the respective entry points, you can see at a glance what, if any, wants you have in common, which of your respective wants are in direct competition with each other, and which individual wants are not contested by either of you.

Proposal language

The other party's initial proposal will be a statement of their ideal position. You can judge the flexibility of their position by the language used: 'I must insist on . . . I was hoping for . . .'

Differing Entry and Exit points

Negotiators normally have different entry points and the question is whether or not there is an overlap in their exit points (see diagram below). For example, if the most the buyer will pay is less than (i.e. does not overlap with) the least the seller will accept, they are unlikely to reach agreement unless one or both changes their exit points. The fact that their entry points are different is not important – we expect negotiators to enter some distance from where they intend to settle.

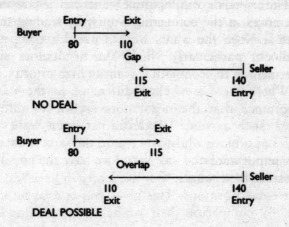

Of the four pieces of information that define each negotiator's ranges – your entry and exit point and the other negotiator's entry and exit point – you only know three of them, namely your own entry and exit points and the other negotiator's entry point. You will not know the exit points of the other negotiator on any of the issues.

Even if the other negotiator tells you what his or her exit point is on an issue you never know for sure it is exactly what they say it is. They may be bluffing; you just do not know for sure.

Competing and Compatible Wants

Competitive wants often dominate the negotiations. You want a high price, the buyer wants a low price; you prefer to limit your liability, they prefer that you accept consequential loss.

Compatible wants are those where it is in your common interest to agree – you both want a workable safety policy, that enables you to protect your employees, them to protect their members.

The existence of compatible wants can help reconcile differences in the competing wants. By trading movement between the wants we can avoid a competitive deadlock, particularly where the negotiators signal agreement in the compatible want of high priority.

Where there is a clear difference in the relative importance that the negotiators ascribe to different wants (such as when I regard a particular want as of High importance whilst you regard the same want as of Low importance and vice versa) we have the possibility of a traded exchange.

Me   You

H   H

M   X   M

L   L

I exchange movement on the want I regard as of low importance, but which you regard as highly important, for your movement on the want I regard as highly important, but which you regard as of lesser importance.

It is in the difference in our priorities for the various wants we are negotiating that enables traded exchanges to take place to arrive at a new solution to the negotiating problem.

New issues emerge in debate

New issues, emerging through the medium of debate, can be those which you have not so far considered, or which are only of interest to the other party. The latter are the most useful; relatively unimportant to you, but essential to them. These wants can be invaluable in subsequent proposing and bargaining and it is vital not to concede them unilaterally. They can form the crucial item in our trade in wants.

What is a proposal?

A proposal is a tentative answer to the question: which wants of the other negotiator might I have to meet if I am to get what I want? Therefore, a proposal is more effective if it is conditional: 'If you give me some of my wants, then I could give you some of your wants.' It conveys the tentative terms upon which you might do business.

The two elements of a proposal

A proposal consists of two elements: the condition and the offer. The condition states what you want from the other negotiator and the offer states what you might trade in return.

Activity 7

What is wrong with the following proposals?

- 'How about I made it £500 instead of £540?'
- 'OK. I'll throw in the gloves and goggles.'
- 'I couldn't go as low as £20,000.'

The first 'proposal' is a question and not an assertive statement. It is unconvincing and in the form of a question. Questions posing as proposals seldom do other than bolster the confidence of the other party and proposals without conditions invite demands for more.

The second 'proposal' is another example of a concessionary and not a conditional proposal. Anything 'thrown in' cannot be worth much to you and as the other party is asked to give nothing in return it will be treated as a 'free gift'.

The third 'proposal' invites the inevitable response: 'how low can you go?'

Make proposals conditional

Proposals are more effective when they are conditional 'If . . . then': 'If you consider my concerns then I will consider your concerns.'

A tentative conditional proposal will give you an advantage by leaving you room to manoeuvre in later stages of the negotiating process. If you concede when proposing, bargaining will be much more difficult.

Condition only

A proposal that consists only of a condition demands that the other negotiator gives in. The statements: 'You will pay in advance' could cause offence by its abruptness and apparent lack of an offer of anything in return.

Offer only

A proposal consisting only of an offer is a unilateral concession to the other party's demands. 'We will give you a discount of 15 per cent' might result in the other side's goodwill, but is more likely to provoke further demands. If you will give 15 per cent for nothing, what else will you concede under real pressure?

VAGUE OR SPECIFIC?

Your condition may be vague or specific, but your offer must always be vague, though expressed firmly:

- 'If you could improve your delivery schedules then I could consider minimum volume orders'
- 'If you could improve your delivery schedules by three days then I could consider minimum volume orders'

Why should proposed offers always be vague?

Why? Because for as long as it is not clear what proposal will be acceptable it is necessary to have some flexibility. The vagueness of the offer does precisely that – it leaves you room for movement without giving in. You offer to 'consider/look at/re-think' the acceptability of the other party's wants, or you might offer to 'find a way to do something about' this or that want.

Degree of flexibility?

Flexibility is the extent to which you are prepared to move from your initial position. Too little flexibility could give the impression that you are unwilling to negotiate at all, causing the other party to abandon negotiations. Alternatively, too much will signal that you are not committed to your position and you will not be taken seriously. The answer is to retain sufficient flexibility to revise your position upwards or downwards when necessary, but always conditionally.

Making Statements

A common behaviour in negotiation, and one which is both important and often neglected, is the making of statements. Statements are neutral when they are not presented argumentatively, and they are not the same as the behaviours of questioning, summarising and signalling. They are not meant to push the negotiation forwards or drag it backwards into argument.

You have an opportunity to make statements when you explain what you want, when you answer questions, or when you make a supporting case for your general position on an issue. They are scene setters and mostly are delivered in measured tones.

You should make statements without comments on the other party's alleged motivations or intentions because these provoke denial and rebuttal and may divert you from your purpose.

Activity 8

What do the following examples of measured statements have in common?

- 'Unless we make a profit we cannot support our customers when they are in difficulty.'
- 'We cannot accede to price increases unless we are convinced of their necessity.'
- 'We can only work with you on this project as long as we are not prohibited from working with other firms on their projects.'
- 'We can only appoint you to a non-exclusive agency under European competition law.'

Statements assist in developing principled stances for presenting your own proposals. Those shown in **Activity 8** are examples of statements that clarify the principle underlying the basis for your consideration of their proposals. You can also develop them as the basis for your proposals:

- 'We operate on principle that while trade unions have a right to exercise their proper functions, as employers we have the right to manage our enterprises.'
- 'Let us be clear that we expect to be paid for the services we provide to your business and you are entitled to pay only for the services that you receive.'
- 'You appear to be saying that we cannot change our distributors or agents unless we receive the permission of our competitors.'

Get the idea? Re-cast proposals or suggestions into a statement of the principle behind them. It will stiffen your resolve and be treated seriously by the other party.

HOW TO MAKE A PROPOSAL

State your proposal. Then stop talking. Make sure you do not interrupt the silence – you could end up making unnecessary concessions or diverting attention from your proposal to your explanations. Silence will put the other negotiator under pressure. You have seized the initiative – it's up to them to justify their contention that your proposal is unacceptable.

Either/or proposal
This is a variation which has certain advantages. By giving the other party a choice between proposals you

reduce the likelihood that they will instantly accept or reject, and by the choices they make you will gain a further insight into their position.

RESPONDING TO A PROPOSAL

You do not expect a 'Yes' to a proposal, although even if you do get a 'Yes' there is still a lot of work to do. You will then be required to specify the actual content of your hitherto vague offer. An affirmative reply to your proposal only suggests that the other party is at least interested in exploring the exchange you have suggested.

Use questions to respond to a proposal

Questions are the most effective response to a conditional proposal, either to question the condition, or to uncover details of the vague offer, clarifying any ambiguities or aspects that are not understood:

- 'If you substantially increase the volume you order, then I will consider offering a discount'
- 'What volume do you have in mind?'

Summarize the proposal

Whether you find the proposal acceptable or not, attempt to summarize it. You need not be concerned that merely talking about the proposal makes it acceptable because nothing is agreed until you say it is agreed.

Beware of saying 'No'

The most common mistake people make is to say 'No' to anything with which they disagree. Not that you should never say 'No' – there are circumstances when 'No' is sufficient – but an instant negative is often counter-productive. They may not consider that you gave their proposal sufficient attention (remember the need for mutual respect). Moreover, an instant 'No' gives insufficient information to discriminate between the absolute 'No', in the sense of 'never' and the relative 'No', in the sense of 'maybe, if there were some changes'.

Don't respond instantly
In fact any instant response – whether a negative or a counter-proposal – is likely to send the wrong signal: i.e. that you are only interested in your own solution, not the other negotiator's contribution.

How to receive a proposal: a summary
Don't interrupt: a free concession often comes at the end of a statement, and will be missed out; you might also cause antagonism. Don't instantly reject a proposal.

CONSIDERED ALTERNATIVE PROPOSAL

A considered alternative proposal is a considered response to the proposed exchange of wants suggested by the other negotiator. It follows consideration of what has been proposed and exploration, by questioning and listening, of the content of their proposal. It is a considered alternative rather than a direct and confrontational counter-proposal because it embodies, where possible, elements of the other negotiator's proposals into your own suggested solution.

Example – your considered alternative proposal
By questioning a proposal for a 15 per cent volume discount for an unspecified increase in the order, it is revealed that they are considering 'perhaps doubling' the

order. While the principle of a volume discount is accepted, your concern may be that you could discount your prices and then find that the increased order does not materialize and, moreover, you might consider that a 15 per cent discount is too high. Having considered the proposal and made a judgment about its worth to you, you could make a considered alternative proposal, such as:

'If you contract to take 150 per cent more volume over the next 12 months, then I would be willing to consider a retrospective volume discount of 10 per cent.'

Example – the other negotiator's response

Perhaps you are willing to reduce the qualifying volume below 150 per cent, to raise the discount above 10 per cent, and to amend the retrospective condition. That would be for them to explore and to make a considered alternative proposal to you, such as:

'If you make it a 10 per cent discount on current invoices up to when I reach last year's order levels, and then 15 per cent on all orders from then on, then I am prepared to accept the final 15 per cent discount is allowed retrospectively.'

MIDDLE GROUND

Somewhere between the two converging considered alternative proposals there is a settlement waiting to be discovered.

In general, you trade things of less value to you than to them, in exchange for things of less value to them than to you. For example, when you are thirsty you exchange money for a drink. You value the money at that moment less than you do the means to quench your thirst. If you did not you would keep your money and forego the drink; the person with the drink values your money more than they value the drink. If they did not they would keep their drink and forego your money. The basis of trade is to exchange the money for the drink, or the drink for the money, with both parties gaining by getting what they want from the transaction.

CHECKLIST FOR PROPOSING

- Proposals are more productive than arguments because arguments cannot be negotiated
- Proposals can advance negotiations
- Proposals can seize the initiative
- Unrealistic proposals divide the negotiators
- Interrupting proposals provokes arguments
- Proposals must address the wants of the parties
- Proposals can be used to initiate responses
- Be firm on generalities, e.g. 'We must have compensation'
- Be flexible on specifics, e.g. 'We suggest £10,000 compensation'
- Do not use unassertive language e.g. 'We hope', 'We like', 'We prefer'. Use strong language, e.g. 'We need', 'We must have', 'We require'
- State your conditions first and be vague or specific
- Follow with your offer and be tentative

Memory joggers
- Don't just complain, propose a remedy
- Open realistically
- Move in small steps
- Invite a response

Common mistakes to avoid

- Complaining but not proposing
- Using unassertive language: 'I'd like', 'We wish'
- Making unconditional offers
- Negotiating with yourself before you meet the other side
- Opening with an unrealistic condition or offer
- Behaving inconsistently in moving your position
- Smothering a proposal in verbage
- Interrupting a proposal
- Assuming the other negotiator's proposal to be set in concrete instead of being open to negotiation

CHAPTER 6

Phase four: bargaining

INTRODUCTION

Bargaining involves making exchanges – giving something up in return for gaining something else. It is the phase of negotiation which can make the difference between a successful and unsuccessful outcome of the process – both parties must pay strict attention to what they are doing in order to avoid making untraded concessions.

There are a number of techniques a negotiator can use to ensure they reach an agreement favourable to their interests.

A bargain conveys the precise terms on which you would settle

A bargain is a specific solution to the negotiating problem: what agreement is acceptable to both of us? A bargain states the precise terms under which you propose to reach agreement, either on a single issue or on all of the issues.

Bargains are always conditional

A fundamental principle of bargaining is to make any

offers conditional. Nothing is ever given away for free –
everything that is conceded must be traded for something else.

APPROACH TO BARGAINING

All bargains should be expressed in a common format:

- If you . . . then I

For example: 'If you agree to this . . . then I will agree to
that.'

The key words are 'if you agree to this . . .' Without
this provision the other negotiator could simply accept
the offer without giving anything in return.

Similarly, the nature and scope of the trade-off that
you suggest will signal the value that you attach to your
offer. It will also show the other negotiator that you
intend to concede nothing unless it is matched by a
similar effort on their part. Without establishing this
conditional approach they may feel that they will have
gained any concessions that you offer as of right, or via
the apparent strength of their position.

If . . . then – pitfall

Not all the ways of saying 'If . . . then' are automatically helpful. For instance, saying: 'If *we* agree to your
demand, then will *you* agree to ours?' Although this
appears to use the 'If . . . then' format it is a question
not a statement. Bargains state the cost of agreement to
the other party and do not merely ask a closed question
that could invite a negative response or prolonged hag-
gling.

CONDITION AND OFFER

Like a proposal, a bargain consists of a condition plus an offer. The condition will specify precisely what you want from the other negotiator, if you are to commit in your offer to any of the other negotiator's own precise wants.

Unlike a proposal, a bargain consists of a precise condition and a precise offer. There is nothing vague about a bargain.

Using the approach we have discussed, a bargain takes the form: 'If you agree to limit compensation for damages to £35,000, then we will issue a credit note to this amount on next year's business.'

Use condition and offer together

A condition on its own is an ultimatum and, as such, is likely to be treated less than favourably. Conversely, an offer on its own is a free gift and is likely to provoke a demand for more of the same. Only a conditional precise offer in the specific format of 'If you . . . then I' can secure agreement without giving in.

Always lead with conditions

When presenting a revised offer you must not forget to match each further offer with an appropriate condition. Negotiators are sometimes so concerned with getting their revised offer right, and putting it across to the other negotiator, that they forget to place conditions upon it.

Any retrospective attempt to introduce such conditions will probably be treated with some suspicion by the other party involved. They will either be unwilling to take the condition seriously – after all, you have already made the offer – or they will regard it as a breach of convention – a 'moving of the goalposts'.

Therefore you should always lead with your conditions. You are then in a position to bargain relative to your stated requirements.

A BARGAIN IS SPECIFIC – IT SEEKS AGREEMENT

When you bargain you are actively seeking agreement. A 'Yes' response to a bargain is a deal. If there were any vagueness about a bargain it would be indistinguishable from a proposal. You can say 'Yes' to a bargain and end the negotiation on the offered conditional terms. In saying 'Yes', you are accepting both the conditions and the offer.

'Yes' concludes the negotiation

When you bargain there is no more ambiguity about what you would exchange for what you want. If they say 'Yes' the negotiation is concluded and apart from writing up the agreement there is nothing more to negotiate about in respect of the offered bargain.

RESPONDING TO A BARGAIN

Your response to a bargain depends on whether you accept or do not accept the offered deal without further negotiation.

Should you elect to accept it, you merely inform the other negotiator of your acceptance in whatever manner is culturally acceptable. Usually, saying 'agreed', or words to that effect, is enough.

Making a conditional counter-bargain

If it is unacceptable in its current form, however, your

best response is to propose a conditional counter bargain containing your amended terms. Arguing is a weak response because it returns you to the midst of the debate phase and is unlikely to produce a revised bargain. You may, nevertheless, return to the debate phase to explore possibilities of movement – by asking further questions or looking for signals as to possible areas of renegotiation.

Using instant counter-bargains

It is quite common for negotiators to propose counter-bargains that amend each other's last conditional offer, without a great deal of additional debate on the merits of their cases. Instant counter-bargains are acceptable in the bargaining phase and have much to commend them in focusing the momentum of the negotiation towards its ultimate conclusion.

EXCHANGE OF PROPOSALS

An exchange of proposals could spark off a run at an attempted bargain. The ease with which negotiators slip from a proposal (vague conditional offer) to a bargain (specific conditional offer) often moves a negotiation to a close in fairly rapid order. By the time negotiators are ready to bargain they should have a fair knowledge of what is likely to be acceptable and how far they have to move to trade for what they want.

APPROACHES TO BARGAINING PROBLEMS

- If they do not accept your bargain, remember that arguing for or against a bargain is usually ineffective

- If they reject your bargain, require them to propose their alternative
- If you reject their bargain try a conditional counter-bargain that changes the conditions or the offer, or both, in your favour
- Iterate towards an agreement

Arguing is a common mistake

The most common mistake is to continue to argue against proposals that you disagree with. By argument alone you miss the opportunity of using a considered alternative proposal – particularly one that incorporates by design elements of the other negotiator's original proposal – to move into the bargaining phase.

Instead of disagreeing in the forlorn hope that they will change their mind on the basis of your arguments alone, you can move them from their current proposal by offering them a precise bargain. This could take the form of: 'If you drop/amend/change your conditions or offer in the following way, then I will improve/alter/change my offer in this way.

When they say 'No!'

Is 'No' ever a proper response to a bargain? Rarely. It gives no information about the relative merits of the proposed bargain. They do not know what parts, if any, you consider potentially acceptable, making it very difficult for them to respond to your 'No'.

Of course, if you oppose absolutely everything about the offered bargain clearly you have a long way to go to reach a settlement!

'No' is too abrupt. It is wholly negative and conveys the impression that you are not committed to seeking a solution. As a tactical ploy it has many weaknesses, not the least being the possible reaction of the other party.

They might break off the negotiations or become highly negative themselves.

Activity 9
When was the last time you had the response of an outright 'No' to one of your proposed bargains? How did you feel about it? More co-operative or less so?

Alternatives to 'No'
You can respond fairly quickly with questions. During the bargaining phase, which is usually near the close of the negotiation, the condition and the offer are explicit and detailed. You should have a pretty clear idea from the debate phase of what is possible under the circumstances.

Attempts to improve the conditions and/or the offer are legitimate alternatives to a blanket 'No'.

Deadlock
Just as a proposal beats a deadlocked debate, so a bargain can unblock a deadlocked proposal.

But all the traps of argument, talking past each other, mis-stating proposals, refusing to address (let alone consider) the other party's interests, failed ploys and narrow vision potentially are present in the bargaining phase. People in the bargaining phase do not only move, ratchet like, forwards and never backwards.

NEGOTIATING SEVERAL ISSUES

Where more than one issue is in contention (the normal case), it is important to abide by two principles:

- Nothing is agreed until everything is agreed
- All issues are linked together

Keep the whole deal together

The first principle effectively guarantees the second. A piecemeal agreement on an isolated issue could leave you short of negotiating room when you reach the later issues. Your problem then would be how to generate room on the outstanding issues without giving in. On the other hand, by keeping the issues linked you have the means to keep the negotiation open until all the issues are covered.

Nothing is agreed until everything is agreed

Hence, by referring to agreement on issue 1 as being provisional, you are able to refer back to issue 1 (or any other issue) as a means of overcoming a disagreement arising on issue 6.

For example: 'We are unlikely to make progress on this issue (6) as it stands, but if you would reassess issue 1 and allow me to make a proposal in respect of them both, I think we could find a way forward.' Objections that issue 1 has been agreed will require you to remind the other negotiator of your provisional, as stated, acceptance of earlier issues. Remember: 'Nothing is agreed until everything is agreed.'

Single issue bargaining and tradables

In a single issue contest any movement by you towards the other party worsens your position and improves theirs; your loss is their gain.

But in most negotiations there is more than one negotiable issue. Even a single issue like the money contains within it many sub-issues.

The amount of money is one issue, when the money is paid is another issue, and how it is paid, in what currency, and through whom are others. Similar issues and sub-issues can be derived for other single negotiable issues.

These are known as the tradables in the deal and looking for tradables – anything that either party has discretion over – is an essential task for the negotiator both in preparation and during the debate and proposal phases to identify as many tradables as you can find. The more tradables the greater your flexibility and the more likely that the settlement will fit yours and the other party's needs.

This task is made easier if you prevent yourself ending up with all issues settled but one that is left over (usually the money). Hence, nothing is agreed until everything is agreed.

Activity 10
List the potential tradables in your business negotiations. If something can be varied in any way then it can become a tradable if at least one party values it.

You do not have to restrict your trading only to the tradables associated with an issue. You can also trade across several unrelated issues. You can propose trading movement on one issue for movement on another by explicitly linking them conditionally.

This can be persuasive when the other party feels that though she has 'lost' something on one issue she has 'gained' at least adequate compensation on another issue.

The logjam breaks as each party considers the net gains and losses from movement across all the negotiable issues, including the tradables within each main issue. This is very different from the certain (and psychic) loss that negotiators feel when considering movement on a single issue only.

The significance of linking issues
This approach could be countered by the apparently logical suggestion that the list of demands, objections,

or requirements etc. should be dealt with one at a time. For one thing, an item-by-item approach has administrative advantages, if only in the sense of an orderly agenda.

Nevertheless you must, on no account, be persuaded that an administrative convenience implies that provisional agreement on issues in a list shuts the door on all further consideration of the issues when there is deadlock on late issues. All the disputed and agreed issues should be linked together in the bargaining phase.

By negotiating each item individually you could be forced to make concessions on each and every point. When you reach the stage of negotiating any issues that remain you may find yourself having nothing left to bargain with.

At this point you will be faced with either: abandoning all hope of reaching an agreement, and shouldering whatever costs this may entail; or seeking authorization to improve your offer and taking the inevitable criticism from your colleagues.

CHECKLIST FOR BARGAINING

- Absolutely firm rule – no exceptions at all, ever: 'Every offer must be conditional'
- Decide what you require in exchange for your offers
- List and place that at the front of your proposal
- Keep all the issues linked and trade off a move on one for a new condition or a move on something else
- Be ready to bring back into contention any previously 'settled' issues if you need negotiating room under pressure of deadlock on a point

Memory joggers
- Remember 'If you . . . then I'
- Never give something for nothing
- Lead with your conditions
- Keep the issues linked

Common mistakes to avoid
- Unconditional offers
- Asking permission to concede using question proposals: 'If I . . . will you?'
- Forgetting to state your conditions
- Separating the offer from the conditions with explanatory comments
- Agreeing to issues one at a time
- Not linking movement on one issue to movement on another

Bargaining possibilities
- They get what they want on your terms
- You get what you want on their terms
- You both get some of what you want on each other's terms
- 'If you've got what the other guy wants, you've got a deal' (Donald Trump)

CHAPTER 7

Agreement

INTRODUCTION

There are two major pressures which a negotiator has to contend with. The first of these stems from the fundamental uncertainty of negotiating: never really knowing whether you are anywhere near the other negotiator's Exit limit. As a result, you delay coming to a decision about what is on offer at any moment just in case there is more you can get. The other pressure urges you to come to an agreement before the other negotiator has the opportunity to 'squeeze' you any further towards your Exit limit.

The longer the negotiations continue the more time you have to extract all the concessions available from them but, by the same token, the longer you negotiate the more time they have to do the same to you.

THE IMPORTANCE OF CLOSING TECHNIQUES

Inexperienced negotiators often find it difficult to know when, or how, to close deals. As a result, they frequently continue negotiations for too long and, in the process, risk conceding further, apparently 'minor', points. When taken as a whole, however, these could represent a substantial additional concession. This situation can be avoided by using the closing techniques given below.

Terminating a negotiation is often difficult
You do not like to say 'Yes' in case you can improve on the other negotiator's current offer; you do not like to continue saying 'No' in case they come up with something you would rather keep out of the discussion. Hence, you dither.

Deciding when to close
It is easier to learn how to close than when to close.

The credibility of your close determines how the other negotiator reacts to it, as they will not know how close you are to your limit.

By closing you are letting the other party know that you do not intend to improve on your current offer and it is in their best interest to reach an agreement with you.

Nevertheless, attempting to close too early can be dangerous: once you have presented your 'best offer', and it has been rejected, you could find yourself trading further expensive concessions later on, plus having to do so in circumstances where your attempt to close too early has damaged your credibility.

Have you achieved what you wanted?
It is best to follow the advice of terminating when you feel that you have achieved what you wanted. Hanging on for more risks something emerging that causes a collapse of the deal. In my experience the greedy often do worse than the needy.

Don't agree too hastily

Being too eager to agree because the other party has inadvertently offered, or appears to have offered to meet all your wildest expectations is not necessarily a sensible course of action either. Your reaction may draw their attention to the fact that they have been over-generous, or may lead them to believe that what they are getting is not worth as much as they thought it was. They may then look for some way to undo the deal, or, if they have already committed to it, they might still create difficulties during its implementation.

SELECTING A METHOD FOR CLOSING

There are several methods of closing (as detailed below), although two – the traded movement close and the summary close – tend to predominate.

Traded movement close

Terminates the bargaining phase by proposing a conditional traded movement to clinch the deal. You must carefully judge the size of movement offered: too big, and they may believe you can be pressurized to concede even more; too small, and it may be too insignificant to bring about acceptance.

Summary close

Remind the other negotiator of the movement you have both made, and highlight the benefits to them of acquiescing to the proposed agreement. Then summarize what has been agreed and how far you have moved, then call for agreement on the terms you have offered.

Make them realize the extent of the effort you have both put into the negotiation and emphasize the opportunity to reach a mutually acceptable agreement. This method is particularly useful where progress has been difficult.

Adjournment close

Summarize as above and suggest an adjournment for each negotiator to consider the merits of agreement on the current terms. Specify the duration of the adjournment (hours, days or weeks).

Adjournment will allow the other negotiator time to reach a considered judgment of the implications of accepting/rejecting the agreement proposed. It also creates the danger that in the adjournment the other party may reconsider its opportunities and use the conditional offer as a benchmark to see if they can improve on it with a third party. If they can, they have the choice of dumping your proposed deal.

'Or else' close

Summarize as above and call for a decision by a specific date, with an explicit statement of the consequences (for both parties) of non-agreement.

This is, of course, an ultimatum: 'Accept the offer or else!' – it is likely to provoke hostility in the other party.

Either/or close

This is a good approach if you are at your budget limits. You present the other negotiator with a choice of alternative agreements and they are free to make a decision between them.

Activity 11

How did a recent negotiation end? Did you come to the close using some version of the bargaining closes shown here? If not, what triggered the final acceptance of the deal?

AGREEMENT CAN BE DANGEROUS!

Agreement to what is on offer is the last step in the negotiating process. It is the outcome towards which all negotiators work. Once it is within your reach, therefore, you feel relief from the tension of the negotiating process and often experience a sense of euphoria. This is a dangerous time. People often believe something was agreed when in fact it was not. Be on your guard. Pay attention to the details of what you agree.

Activity 12
Observe how a negotiation affects the body language and behaviours of negotiators during the end phase.

Watch for the negotiators sitting up, moving closer and leaning over their side of the table, maintaining eye contact, paying attention to what is said and generally behaving with barely concealed excitement. Mutual euphoria generally produces co-operative gestures; mutual depression generally produces frustration and slumped bodies pushed away from the table.

Agree what you have agreed
It is absolutely essential that both parties agree what they have agreed with each other before they leave the table, and that the agreement is recorded in an acceptable manner. This is the way to pre-empt subsequent confusion, disagreement and hostility.

Each issue which has been subject to negotiation should be summarized, and the summary agreed between the parties. Any terms that could be subject to differences in interpretation should be defined. (For example, generalized terms such as: reasonable, adequate, sufficient, etc.)

For less formal negotiations, a letter documenting

the settlement reached should be sent by you as soon as possible after the close of negotiations.

DISAGREEMENT OVER INTERPRETATION

The consequences of not confirming what you have agreed, even with people you know and trust, can be horrendous. Any form of dispute which arises later on, perhaps during the implementation of the negotiated agreement, could imply malpractice on your part, even if you are innocent. Naturally the other negotiator will dispute an interpretation of the alleged agreement that they have retrospectively discovered to be to their detriment. Whether openly stated or not, doubts as to each party's good faith and real intentions will be raised.

Convincing somebody that they really did agree to what has turned out to be a disadvantageous clause in a contract, even if brilliantly presented, may leave them feeling resentful. It may also leave you with the suspicion that they have been trying to take advantage of you, and neither outcome is good for your relationship.

Agreements should be completely clarified at the negotiation stage
To avoid the possibility of later discord, confirm in detail what you agreed and clarify any potentially contentious points before you leave the negotiating table.

Negotiate what you agreed
If the summary of what you believe has been agreed to does cause conflict, then it is necessary to re-open negotiations until you can find an agreement. A failure to reach full agreement before you implement a deal is as

disastrous as trying to implement a deal which has not been agreed to at all.

CHECKLIST FOR CLOSING AND AGREEING

- Decide where and when you intend to stop trading
- Is it credible? Is it too soon?
- Have they identified or signalled that an improved offer on your part on some item will trigger agreement to the package? (If not, you must get all of their objections out before trading any more offers.) If 'Yes', consider the traded movement close
- Lead with the summary close and then try the traded movement close or vice versa
- If you are going for a 'final offer' are you serious or is it a bluff? Remember, a final offer increases in credibility the more formal it is, the more senior the person delivering it, the more public the audience, the more specific it is and the more specific the time for acceptance. Bluffing 'final offers' can destroy credibility in the current negotiations and in subsequent ones. Do not try to force a 'final offer' under emotional pressure
- Remember: 'adjournment' and 'or else' closes have a greater risk in them than traded movement and 'summary closes' (and 'either/or' closes)
- If the close has succeeded: what has been agreed?
- Detail the agreement
- List all points of explanation, clarification, interpretation and understanding
- Try to prevent them from leaving until an agreed summary has been recorded
- If there is disagreement on an alleged agreement recommence the negotiation until agreement is reached again

- If the agreement is oral, send a written note to the other party of what you believe was agreed immediately after the meeting

Common mistakes to avoid
- Inability to terminate bargaining
- Giving away concessions in the euphoria of the closing moments
- Misjudging final offers
- Bluffing with a 'final' offer
- Unconditional closing concessions
- Making large closing concessions
- Not summarizing what has been agreed
- Making inappropriate threats using the 'or else' close or the 'either/or' close
- Not recording what has been agreed in an acceptable form
- Trying to 'cheat' when recording the alleged agreement

CHAPTER 8

Styles of negotiation

INTRODUCTION

We do not negotiate in a vacuum. Just because we happen to be deciding something, neither of us need attempt to bargain. You might seek to force me to capitulate. Neither of us need believe in 'fairness'. You might attempt to exploit me by smart sales techniques, or by playing on my ignorance, or by threatening me with awful consequences if I resist you.

Where does this leave the negotiator, the person who wants to trade to arrive at a solution when up against somebody else who does not?

The style dimension
Negotiators are divided between those who want to take something for nothing (the RED stylists) and those who prefer to give something for nothing (the BLUE stylists).

The style dimension is a continuum, with aggressive Red stylists at one end and assertive Blue stylists at the other. In between the extremes there are varying shades of redness and blueness.

Red stylists believe that negotiations work best for them by:

- Seeing all negotiations as 'one-off' activities
- Winning through domination
- Believing that more for them means less for you
- Using bluffs, ploys, 'dirty tricks' and coercion to get their own way
- Taking something for nothing

Activity 13
When was the last time that you made a Red demand (taking something for nothing) on somebody? Recollect the exact words you used. Why did you think it appropriate to do so?

Blue stylists believe that negotiations work best for them by their being liked:
- Seeing all negotiations in their long-term contexts
- Succeeding through submission
- Believing that more for them is good enough for you
- Avoiding manipulative techniques
- Giving something for nothing or very little

Activity 14
When did you last make a Blue offer (giving something for nothing) on somebody? What circumstances made you do so? Were you intimidated? Or is giving your normal inclination?

In practice, the clash between Red and Blue styles leads to varying outcomes, none of them optimal. Both Red and Blue styles are not advised and negotiators must develop an alternative, which we call Purple.

Varying outcomes

A negotiator can be intimidated into submission by an overtly aggressive Red stylist.

The submissive Blue negotiator in practice gives something for nothing – they give up what the other negotiator wants to take and get nothing back in return for it. They are so determined to reach an agreement that they sacrifice their own wants to secure it. They fear failure more than they fear exploitation.

A negotiator can sometimes achieve something for nothing by stealth and by hiding their Red intentions.

These people are covert Red stylists. They exploit either by design or by accident – they cannot resist the opportunity to get something for nothing.

The assertive Purple negotiator, however, always aims to secure agreement by trading something for something.

In different contexts you might on occasion display behaviour from more than one version of a style. For example:

- Whenever you make an unconditional offer you are being submissive
- Whenever you make a unilateral demand, with no offer of anything in return, you are being aggressive
- When you exploit somebody because you cannot resist the temptation, you are being covert

Thus you require a method of dealing with all of these versions of Red and Blue styles. But you must recognize that while some people are predominantly of one distinct style or another (it is not difficult to spot an aggressive negotiator!) the majority of people with whom you will negotiate may not be so obvious in their style preferences and might switch between them depending on how they read the situation and your style.

Activity 15
Think of a recent experience in which you behaved sometimes Red and sometimes Blue. Can you recollect why you behaved this way?

DIFFICULT AGGRESSIVE NEGOTIATORS

You are bound to feel at least some of the time that almost all other negotiators are being difficult to some degree – they do not agree with your solution and stubbornly persist in presenting their own. Most of the time we manage to rise above our impatience.

But we do have to deal with people who choose to behave in an extremely difficult Red fashion beyond the temporary irritations of our discovering that they are not overly enthusiastic about our solutions. These people are usually aggressive, bad mannered and threatening.

The problem is that you want to negotiate and they do not. Their solution requires you to give in to them by giving them what they want (all of it) and foregoing anything in return.

Activity 16
When did you last meet a really difficult Red style negotiator? How did you respond to his or her intimidation? Was it a pleasant experience?

Break the connection between winning and intimidation
Many negotiators behave aggressively, because they know that the submissive submit to aggression.

Many of them behave aggressively because they confuse aggression with toughness. They adopt aggressive behaviour because they know of no other method that would get them what they want. And because they find that other people submit to their aggressiveness, they conclude that the aggressive win and therefore they become aggressive whenever they want something.

Activity 17

Why do you think difficult Red style negotiators behave in the way they do? Is it from psychological quirks in their personalities? Or is it because they believe that behaving in this way tends to get them what they want?

You have to break the connection between winning and intimidation. If you do not do this, your submission reinforces the high success rate for those who win through intimidation.

You must base your behaviour on two principles:

1. No submission to intimidation, bullying or threats;
2. No agreement unless it is based on:
- The merits of their case
or
- Trading something that you want from them

If their case has merits (you are in the wrong on something) it is pointless trying to defend the indefensible – it only fuels their aggression. How you put it right depends on context, but certainly an indicated willingness to put it right is a minimum step towards doing so.

For example, an irate customer can at least be calmed down by asserting:

- That you apologize for the stress you have caused them
- That you will listen to what they have to say
- That you intend to put the matter right

In the absence of any merits in their case (which of course requires that you listen to what they have to say), or a willingness on their behalf to consider a trade, you will steadfastly refuse to be bullied.

Match?

When confronted by a difficult negotiator: you can style match, but it is risky.

In matching you respond in similar vein to the difficult negotiator's behaviour.

Activity 18

Think back to a time when you have matched Red style behaviour. What was the dispute about? Did your matching strategy or response work?

The danger is that the aggressive negotiator interprets your counter-stance merely as you being aggressive too (he misses the message about merits or trading as your preferred solutions) and concludes that it needs an 'extra push' from him to force you into submission. He escalates the pressure and you escalate your response.

This risks a dispute about 'who started it', which blocks progress in the negotiations (even precludes negotiations at all) because the answer is lost in the confusing layers of mutual insults and threats and counters.

The outcome depends on what happens next after your bout of style matching.

You style match to avoid submitting to aggressive pressure, but when doing so you must leave wide open the alternative route to a settlement through negotiation. 'It does not have to be this way' is a useful common refrain.

Contrast?

Style contrasting is also risky because a contrasting response to aggression could be perceived by the difficult negotiator as evidence of your submission and a justification for their aggression.

Instead of responding in kind to their ill-mannered and abusive behaviour you should:

- Speak more quietly than they do
- Speak more slowly than they do
- Give way to their interruptions – but pause for a few seconds each time they finish
- Not join in bouts of swearing
- Not get dragged into attack against ascribed motives
- Avoid defending yourself against ascribed motives
- Ignore all threats

Activity 19

Think back to a time when you contrasted Red style behaviour. What was the dispute about? Did your contrasting strategy or response work?

Of course, contrasting responses like these run the risk of misinterpretation. You could be thought of as submissive. But the contrary impression depends on what else you do in association with your contrasting style.

You should repeat the statement – having gained their attention, which will probably mean that you have to repeat it more than once – that you will not submit to pressure but only to the merits of their case or to the exchange principle.

For a contrasting style to have impact, it is absolutely essential that you respond instantly, positively and specifically, and without rancour for past insults etc., to any and all of the trading moves that they make. This is critical. Delaying your response, being mealy mouthed about it, hankering after punishment of them for their misdeeds etc., endangers the impact of your message. This is particularly true when they make a small signal of a change in tack in the midst of their aggressive activities.

As for their Red moves, you have nothing to gain from responding to them other than to say 'no'. You must affirm whenever appropriate the two principles on which you will agree to a solution (merits of the case and trading).

Your assertive Purple message will eventually prevail (it is the only way they can do business with you and you will do business with them).

To help you to hold the line in what is a most difficult and trying situation, remember that toughness is not a synonym for shouting abuse, threatening and intimidation. Toughness is based on an absolute and patient firmness of purpose. Only ever to bargain conditionally: 'you will get nothing from me unless and until I get something from you.'

HOW TO DEAL WITH COVERT RED NEGOTIATORS

The main problem is that most covert Red stylists do not start off with the intention of cheating you (some do, of course). The majority of occasions when you are exposed to a covert Red who will cheat you are when otherwise normally honest people find it impossible to resist the temptation to do so. The opportunity to cheat appears without warning and, faced with a safe 'steal', they submit to the temptation.

Opportunity to cheat

The fact is that you do not know for certain whether a negotiator will exploit you. They are unaware themselves of how they will act if they are given an opportunity to exploit you.

This puts you at a disadvantage but this is one disadvantage which is an integral aspect of the business of negotiation. If it is of any comfort, it also puts everybody else at a disadvantage – they do not know if you will be tempted to cheat them. Nobody knows for sure how they will react if an opportunity arises with some person they are dealing with – we all have the potential to be tempted into being covert Red stylists in certain circumstances, and we almost certainly all have succumbed to that temptation in the past.

Hence, you could be dealing with an apparent assertive Purple negotiator behaving just like you.

This person may intend from the start to exploit you or may be unable to resist the temptation. If they intend to exploit you there are precious few clues, if any, in their behaviour because their intentions are deliberately hidden (that is why they are covert). In the latter case, they cannot help it when the opportunity arises, perhaps on this single occasion. Their behaviour up to that moment is absolutely honest and above-board but they switch to the covert Red role without revealing what they are doing.

Causes of the covert Red problem

Your problem can only arise if you relax and forget to apply the exchange principle based on conditionality.

If you believe that you are dealing with another ethical negotiator, you might demonstrate a co-operative tendency in your style and inadvertently expose yourself to exploitation.

If you reveal your expectations – even your interests – believing that it is safe to do so with this person (who is clearly not an aggressive Red stylist) you might create the irresistible temptation for them to take advantage.

If you carelessly offer movement on the implicit understanding that they will reciprocate, that could be the invitation for them to strike.

Examples include:

- You reveal that you desperately require their services – to exploit you they can increase their Entry price
- You let them know that your budget is in surplus with no virement provisions – they can take advantage of your predicament by quoting a premium price despite your early payment
- You confess that your cash flow is desperate – they strike swiftly by insisting (with regrets) on advance payment

Most covert Red responses are accepted by their victims because it is easier to become a submissive Blue, particularly as the covert Red usually dress up their response in such a way as to convince you that they are genuine.

How to test for covert Red with signals
Basically by never becoming deluded that it is safe to reveal your vulnerabilities to everybody and by never dropping the stance that everything but everything is traded and nothing but nothing is conceded.

Among the assertive skills that you must practise is the use of signals to test for covert Red intentions in people who might be tempted to cheat.

A signal addresses the major strategic question of all negotiators: How can we indicate a willingness to move without it being interpreted as our giving in? Signals

indicate a willingness to consider some form of movement only if that movement is not interpreted as you
giving in.

- From demanding full compensation you signal that
  you require *some* compensation
- From rejecting a demand as impossible you signal
  that it would be *contrary to normal policy*
- From rejecting a general principle you signal a willingness to discuss specific instances where it might be
  applicable

The key is in how the other negotiator responds to your
signal. If they rubbish it, they reveal themselves as Red
stylists. But even if they respond positively to your signal
you still cannot be sure about them. Suppose their
clarification questions lead you into further disclosures
rather than into a positive response from themselves?

In short, no matter what they appear to be, you
never know if they are genuine traders or potentially
covert Red exploiters.

Responding to your signals might reveal them to be
Red stylists (seeking something for nothing) but it will
not prove beyond doubt that they are not. They might
finesse something for nothing from you if you carelessly
give them the chance.

The exchange principle
What you do in a negotiation is critical to the outcome.
You need not always be a victim of Red styles. The
answer to Red style behaviour lies in your application of
the exchange principle.

Every one of us has a Red side because if somebody
offers us what we want for nothing, we will surely take
it, and taking something for nothing is a Red style

behaviour. When we get something for nothing no exchange takes place.

Now suppose we make a proposal that only consists of stating what we want and offer nothing in return to the other negotiator.

What is the nature of our proposal? Surely an aggressive Red stylist's attempt to get something for nothing!

Most of us have a submissive Blue side because there are occasions upon which we would certainly offer something and expect nothing in return when motivated by love, terror, tiredness, altruism, etc.

Now suppose we make a proposal that only consists of an offer (which gives them what they want) and requires nothing at all from the other negotiator.

What is the nature of this proposal? Surely a submissive Blue stylist's free gift concession giving away something for nothing! And when we give something for nothing no exchange takes place.

Thus, these types of proposal by themselves identify the aggressive Red or the submissive Blue stylist. Separately they are unhelpful to a negotiator – Red demands provoke resentment if not resistance, Blue offers provoke exploitation.

But the exchange principle combines the Red demand with the Blue offer and together they become the foundation of sound negotiation practice.

Combine condition and offer together into a conditional proposal and the assertive Purple negotiator is totally protected whatever the style coming across the table – overt, covert or submissive.

Analogously, the two elements sodium and chlorine are poisonous to humans if ingested separately, but they are also the foundation of life (salt) when ingested together.

A Purple style!

Think of the assertive conditional proposal as a Purple style (a bit of Red and a bit of Blue – the proportions depending on the terms of a proposed deal).

Conditional proposals consisting of your Red conditions and your Blue offers are Purple defences against any Red plays, whether openly aggressive or covertly threatening.

* Always use conditional Purple proposals (IF you ... THEN I) to be assertive

Your imposed conditionality asserts that they cannot get what they want from you without you getting what you want from them.

The exchange principle conditionally stated:

* Blocks aggressive Red stylists from intimidating you into submission for as long as you apply it
* Does not exploit the submissive Blue because being used to giving things away for nothing they get something back through your conditional offer
* Paralyses the covert Red because if they challenge the exchange principle (you must get something back for what you offer them) they would have to reveal their Red 'something for nothing' intentions which the *covert* cannot do
* Is acceptable in form at least if not in its contents by genuine assertive Purple negotiators because they apply the same Purple exchange principle themselves in their negotiations

CHECKLIST FOR NEGOTIATION STYLES

- 'More for me means less for you' is a Red style
- 'Less for me means more for you' is a Blue style
- 'More for me means more for you' is a Purple style
- Aggressive Red stylists take something for nothing
- Submissive Blue stylists give something for nothing
- Covert Red stylists finesse something for nothing
- Assertive Purple stylists trade something for something
- Against aggressive Red stylists:
    assert that you will not submit to intimidation
    agreement is only possible if based on
        either the merits of the case or the
        exchange principle
- Apply the Purple exchange principle to all proposals (IF you . . . THEN I) to protect yourself from aggressive and covert Red negotiators

Common mistakes to avoid
- Being inflexible when dealing with styles
- Submitting to aggressive Red behaviour
- Failing to test for covert Red responses to signals
- Forgetting to link your Red conditions with your Blue offers

CHAPTER 9

The role of ploys

INTRODUCTION

For a lot of people negotiation is about 'dirty tricks', ploys and gambits, which are sometimes confused with 'tactics'. However, much of the advice available on ploys and tricks is unhelpful.

While learning about manipulative approaches to negotiation has something to commend it – because any experience of business negotiation will show numerous ploys being tried upon you – refining your manipulation skills has little to recommend it. But because negotiation is an unscripted interaction with no rules, no appeals and no comebacks, mistakenly it appears on the surface that a manipulative approach is the dominant one and something you must become adept in quickly if you are to do well.

The fact remains that manipulative approaches can be counter-productive if you confuse identifying what some people might try to do to you in a negotiation with what you must learn to do to them.

Books, videos and seminars that teach tactical manipulation suffer from at least five drawbacks:

- You forget the appropriate ploy for the situation
- You apply the wrong ploy for the situation
- The situation was not covered in the programme
- Ploys undermine relationships
- Every ploy has a counter

This could leave you bereft of ideas when trying to develop a negotiation plan or trying to conduct a negotiation.

Does a chapter on manipulative ploys contradict the above? Not in this context. There is a big difference between identifying some of the manipulative ploys that may be used against you and encouraging you to become a manipulative negotiator.

A ploy identified by you in the course of a negotiating exchange is a ploy neutralized. Moreover, the fact that you realize they are attempting to manipulate you should alert you to their Red intentions.

Role of manipulative ploys

All manipulative ploys have a single aim, namely to influence the perception you have of their power relative to your own.

Your perceptions of their power and your expectations of the likely outcome of the negotiation are linked together:

- The less power relative to you that you perceive them to have, the greater your expectation that the outcome will be favourable to you
- The more power that you perceive them to have relative to you, the less your expectation that the outcome will be favourable to you

The manipulative negotiator strives to influence your perceptions of their power relative to yours because by doing so he can directly influence what you expect to result from the negotiation.

If you perceive your power to be

- Non-existent in the situation, you are likely to give in (which happens everytime you visit a supermarket to buy some groceries)
- Balanced with theirs, you are likely to trade
- Overwhelming, you are likely to impose compliance on them (why negotiate if they have no options?)

Activity 20
Who among your colleagues or clients do you consider to have more power than you? Try to describe the sources of their alleged power over you. How real are these sources and how do they manifest themselves? Are they assumptions on your part or carefully cultivated images on theirs?

STAGES OF MANIPULATION

All manipulative ploys can be assigned predominantly to three main stages in a negotiation:

- Dominating
- Shaping
- Closing

Negotiations generally follow the above sequence.

DOMINATING

In the dominance stage, the manipulator works to dominate you and the proceedings. If he manages to take over the negotiations in this way he can exert great psychological pressure on you. Knowing that this is his purpose should arm you against being taken in by the onslaught.

He might:

• Insist on pre-conditions before negotiating

You must decide whether you are willing to accept the pre-conditions. You can assert that 'nothing is ruled in and nothing is ruled out', that you would find it difficult to make progress with 'one arm tied behind your back', or that you have a counter-set of pre-conditions which are chosen to circumscribe his room for manoeuvre.

• Declare some issues non-negotiable

Issues that are claimed to be non-negotiable can be divided into two: those that are genuinely non-negotiable and those that are motivated by an attempt to weaken your stance.

Where there is some pressing emotional reason for them making some issues non-negotiable, you can assert your belief that the issues should be a part of the eventual deal, but to assist the exploration of what both of you want you are willing to have these issues set to one side for the moment. Depending on progress on the other issues you can raise the non-negotiable issues at a later time on the grounds that they are the only remaining obstacles to an overall agreement.

• Attempt unilaterally to determine the agenda, its order and the timing

Seizing control of the agenda (what can be discussed and the order in which issues are discussed) is a common manipulative device, and not just in negotiations. The difference between negotiations and routine meetings ensures at least a base for resisting this type of manipulation.

Nothing can really be negotiated without the consent of both parties and agreeing what to negotiate and in what order is a necessary part of a negotiation taking place at all. Where the manipulator scores with this ploy it is usually by default.

- Behave in an aggressive Red style

The aggressive Red style can be tackled using the methods in Chapter 8, as can the use of threats of sanctions. There is little point in responding to threats, especially with counter threats, as this feeds the emotional commitment of the aggressive person. One of the most successful techniques for dealing with threats is to ignore them and with deadlines it is not to acknowledge them.

- Disdainfully dismiss you, your products, your business, your views

The dismissal of you, your products, your business, your beliefs, etc. is an attempt to provoke you into anger or to undermine whatever power you feel you have. Again, by remembering that the purpose of the manipulator's behaviour is to affect your perceptions of the power balance, you can disarm the manipulative ploy by not letting it get through to you.

- Try to intimidate you with props (plush offices, evidence of power, humiliating circumstances for your meeting, keeping you waiting, etc.)

As for intimidation through props, you can cope with them by remembering that 'all that glitters is not gold'. It is when you take on board the subliminal message – this negotiator is too rich and powerful for me to expect too much – that you are making your most serious concession, especially if you start to negotiate with yourself and lower your sights.

SHAPING

In the second stage of negotiation the manipulator works to shape the deal in his favour. Most deals can be cut numerous ways and by shaping each aspect of the deal the manipulator is picking up benefits – often without giving anything in return – that could more appropriately be held on to or traded for something else.

Some common ploys include:

'Tough guy/soft guy'

It does not require two people to play this ploy. It can be as easily (and less obviously) played by one person. He is on your side, he says, but he has people to report to who do not see you in the same light. However, if you give him something here and something there, he will have a better chance of getting the deal past them.

If you believe him, you cut here and there and over there. The deal shapes up into a one-way street – for his benefit not yours.

You can counter with your own 'tough-nice guy' routine – you too have difficult people to please, hence you need something back for any moves that you make.

You can also reveal your knowledge of the ploy, perhaps humorously, and refuse any movement without a trade.

Activity 21

Recall recent examples of anybody trying some version of the tough guy/soft guy ploy on you. When did you last use it on someone else?

Salami

Shaping by cutting thin slices at a time. Unable to get you to move the whole hog in one go, they get you to agree a little movement here and there. Once that is agreed they expand on the movement they have gained.

You can simply salami back – this little movement costs them this little amount, that extended (bigger) movement costs them this bigger amount.

When a deal is being implemented, salami can take on a vicious form, sometimes called the 'nibble'. Here the other negotiator tries to bend the deal by nibbling away at the conditions they did not like at the time.

For example, you thought they had agreed to 30 days payment but they keep taking 40 days to pay. Over time the nibbles get out of control and establish legitimacy because what started off as a tiny nibble can become a permanent and expensive shift in the terms of the deal, and by precedent very difficult to reverse.

The best thing to do with nibbles is to stamp on them immediately they appear, no matter how small the initial transgression. If they agree to pay in 30 days, require a condition that failure to meet 30 days incurs a penalty. If they have no intention of nibbling they will not demur at a penalty – if they do, you have been warned.

Add-on

The possibility of an add-on ploy is always present. You thought the price was inclusive but once you agree to the price, add-ons spring up like weeds. It's extra for this and extra for that. The true cost mounts, which is particularly disconcerting when the add-ons are revealed afterwards when you need some service that you thought was included in the deal.

The add-on is the special favourite of the covert Red negotiator. It can turn a moderately lucrative deal into a virtual licence to collect money. Be wary is the best advice. Always ask for a clear statement of what exactly is included in the proposed deal and what is excluded. 'What do I get for my money?' is a potent anti-add-on preventative counter.

Activity 22
When was the last time you were a victim of the 'add-on' ploy? Did you realise at the time what was happening or did it become apparent only later?

Mother Hubbard
They love you and your product but cannot reach the price and there is no way round their budget constraint. The cupboard is bare, etc. When done convincingly, you re-shape your Exit terms to secure the deal. They get what they want. You get less than you expected.

Counters are difficult – you can test the constraints, for example. But it is probably better to decide early on that if you can make a deal with this negotiator, fine, but if you can't you are perfectly relaxed about not doing any deal on worse than your Exit terms. It is always bad business to cross a bottom line in hot pursuit of an order.

Russian Front
Two lousy alternatives are presented to you, one so horrendous (during World War II it was 'go to the Russian Front') that you will do (almost) anything else to avoid it. A powerful deal shaper ploy that can gob smack you right down to your bottom line (and across it).

Well chosen Russian Fronts are really difficult to counter. 'Reduce your audit fees, or we go out to tender' is currently terrorizing usually sensible accountants. If you believe they will implement the Russian Front to go out to tender, you will cut your fees and by doing so you demonstrate the potency of the ploy and increase the likelihood of repeated Russian Front ploys.

Generating other options is the only sensible response to situations where you are vulnerable to Russian Front ploys.

This selection of shaping ploys does not exhaust the library of them practised by manipulative negotiators. Fortunately, for every ploy there is a counter, but the best defence is to identify the ploy and neutralize its impact on your expectations.

Activity 23
Have you been Russian Fronted recently? What happened? Which option did you choose?

CLOSING

In the final closing stage the Red style manipulator works to close the deal on his terms. He uses time pressure frequently, playing on some notional deadline common to you both or credible to you.

There is also the problem that because one of the important costs of negotiation is the time they take, which prevents you doing other things, the plausibility of getting the deal settled quickly is persuasive.

Rushed deals are bad deals. If somebody is hustling you to close, it might be because the deal suits them as it stands more than it suits you.

For example, he might:

Demand that you split the difference

This gets you halfway across the gap between you both and has a pressing, though spurious, logic about it. If you both move halfway then what could be a fairer compromise? That depends on the nature of the gap between you. Has the manipulator arrived at the gap by falsely padding his Entry position, while you were less devious and are closest to your Exit?

If the pressure to secure the deal accompanies the 'split the difference' ploy, it can prove irresistible. To avoid the ploy try to work in gaps that are not easily split. A gap of 10 is easily conceived of 5 each; a gap of 11.3 is not so obviously divided.

Claim it is 'Now or Never'

'There is a tide in the affairs of men . . .' Whether it really is the last chance to secure a deal is a question worth asking. The context might suggest otherwise. You can only judge the circumstances as you see them. One question to ask is: Why? Their answers might give you a clue to the credibility of the claim.

Threaten with the 'Or Else' close

Echoes of the Russian Front applied to the closing stage. Depends on the content of the 'or else' part of the threat. If credible you must make a choice. Perhaps you should be generating options during a negotiation that give you negotiating room? The more options that you have the stronger the position.

By identifying the likely ploys (and there are many more than the selection quoted above) you can win the battle to influence your perceptions. If you know what he is about it makes it easier either to:

- Counter (every ploy has a counter)
- Ignore (any ploy is weakened by being ignored)

If your perceptions are uninfluenced by the manipulator you can concentrate on negotiating the issues.

CHECKLIST FOR MANIPULATIVE PLOYS

- All ploys have counters
- A ploy recognized is a ploy disarmed
- Ploys are to be avoided in the interests of longer term relationships
- Ploys aim to influence your perceptions of their power
- Your expectations of the outcome are influenced by your perceptions of their powers
- Check out changes in your perceptions
- Which of the three stages are you in: dominating, shaping, closing?

Common mistakes to avoid
- Ploy, gambits, dirty tricks and dishonesty

CHAPTER 10

Negotiating difficult disputes

INTRODUCTION

Intractable disputes are unlikely to be solved by negotiation – which is why they are intractable. But not all disputes – even some bitter ones – need become intractable. It depends on what the parties do once the dispute is recognized.

There is a continuum running from giving in when faced with a dispute through to using violence to force them to give in. In between there are many alternatives to violence. The parties themselves can attempt to resolve the dispute by private discussion, negotiation, mediation and problem solving. They can appeal to other private third parties for arbitration or for a command decision.

Beyond private parties there are public bodies – the law courts, the government and international agencies – who can settle disputes peacefully. And all signatories of the United Nations Charter have agreed to accept restrictions on their otherwise inalienable right to settle disputes violently.

The three components of dispute resolution are power, right and interests. Power in this context is coercion. Rights are independent standards of fairness supported by law or social conventions. Interests are perceived needs, concerns and fears. These components are all pervasive; they are present in all disputes.

Most disputes are settled amicably between the private parties without resorting to litigation or violence.

The private settlement of disputes is often time consuming – a major cost of negotiation, for example, is the time it takes – but the costs of private settlement are less costly than litigation or violence.

Some business sectors have endemic dispute relationships. In construction, for example, main contractors drive down prices for work from sub-contractors (often using aggressive Red ploys); the sub-contractors, to make a profit, often skimp on performance (using covert Red ploys); the main contractors, to avoid fraud, delay payments to sub-contractors until they have checked everything; to survive the sub-contractors skimp on their work. The result is an industry riddled with contentious claims for extra work done (and contentious people pursuing them) and counter-claims for non-performance (and stubborn people resisting them), both of which wind their way slowly through expensive arbitration and legal procedures.

CONFLICT ESCALATION

Disputes can escalate from a difference of opinion over a problem into a major crisis. What begins with some low-scale anxiety ends with bitter feelings of revenge.

The deadening spiral of conflict escalation is at the root of most intractable disputes. Once the problem emerges (perhaps as seen by one affected party) it can pass into a partisan assertion of one group's right over another's. Sides are taken and those who feel the strongest whip up the fears and anxieties of those likely to be influenced.

Polarization leads to militant hostility to people holding a different view, including people from within the affected group who are cast as 'traitors', 'spies' and 'enemies'. Soon all restraint is lost. Moderate appeals, and moderate people, are pushed aside as being 'soft' on the issues.

Threats escalate as perceptions of what is realistically possible become unrecognizably distorted. The original issue is now shrouded in the history of the relationship of the disputing parties. Whatever one did or did not do, it is impossible to separate the issue from the behaviour of the parties.

Intractability reigns, perhaps to the mutual destruction of both parties.

Activity 24

Select an intractable problem from world affairs that you know about, where the parties have passed through all the stages of conflict escalation to that of bitter stalemate and mutual destruction. At what point in the past could the parties have been saved from the mutual destruction that now reigns over them? How might the intractable problem now be unravelled?

INTERESTS

Interests are fundamental to the negotiator's quest to resolve a difficult dispute. Interests express the needs, concerns and fears of the parties. They are what motivates you to want something. Behind all of your wants in a negotiation stand your interests.

More complex disputes cannot be settled solely by addressing the expressed wants of the parties (and it can take some effort even to uncover other people's wants). This is especially true when they have many competing wants because this reflects the fact that they may have competing interests.

As with wants, some interests are competitive, some are compatible. The task is to uncover them. Leaving them hidden or unregarded removes the chance of using revealed interests to promote a settlement.

THE NEGOTIATOR-AS-MEDIATOR

Mediation usually involves some form of impartial intervention by a neutral third party who cannot impose a settlement but can assist the parties to secure one.

Mediators are often used when the negotiations cannot close the gap between them by their own efforts. Basically, the mediator goes behind the public stances of the negotiators, confidentially assesses their interests and finds out their Exit positions on the issues, where there are sufficient overlaps or closeness of issues and wants to suggest that a mutually acceptable settlement is possible, the mediator recommends that they try again.

Negotiators find it difficult to rise above the fray when head-to-head in a dispute and for practical reasons there are just not enough mediators to go round, even assuming both parties would consider using a mediator's services or could afford to do so.

The negotiator who understands the process of negotiation and the appropriate approach to difficult negotiators can engage in the unusual role of the negotiator-as-mediator.

The negotiator as a mediator differs from the normal mediator. For a start, the negotiator is hardly impartial and neutral. They are partisan to their own wants and interests. They cannot expect to get behind the public stances of the other negotiator, nor will they be able to receive confidential briefings on the other negotiator's Exit positions.

But faced with a dispute that is heading towards deadlock, if not quite intractability, the negotiator can adapt some techniques of the mediator and apply them to search for a way towards a settlement with or without the other negotiator's knowledge.

To undertake this task, however, the negotiator has to adopt certain attitudes to the role of the negotiator-as-mediator. In particular the negotiator-as-mediator must accept that:

- Both parties have legitimate interests that are important for them
- A solution meets as many of the interests of each side as is practicable
- Interests unlike wants may be re-prioritised but not traded
- There is likely to be more than one solution that could satisfy both parties
- Some interests will be competing and others will be compatible

This approach helps the negotiator-as-mediator to rise above the fray without compromising his role as a negotiator.

HIDDEN INTERESTS

Getting negotiators to reveal their wants can be difficult enough. Getting them to reveal their interests is equally hard. This is not necessarily a case of the negotiator being difficult.

They may not know what their interests are. They may not be used to expressing their interests or formulating them in any conscious sense. Why should they? Our wants express what we want, our interests why we want it. And most of us do not examine our motives for what we want or realise that we have motives.

Others may deliberately hide their interests either because they are embarrassed of them or because they hope to gain advantage by not revealing them.

Teachers claiming wage increases seldom do so on the basis that they want the higher living standards enjoyed by others. They usually present wage claims as an investment in the future of our children. Others might manoeuvre against a position on some excuse when they are really against it because it will disadvantage them in some way. For example, a person might lead a campaign against something ostensibly on its merits when in fact they are jealous of the person initiating the project and the promotion they might gain from it being successful.

The most common reason for failure to reveal interests is the misconception that what they want is actually the correct expression of their interest. Inflexible defences of positions usually are brought about by seeing inflexibility as an interest when in fact it is merely a position. Shifting negotiators to look beyond their inflexible defence of positions to examine their interests is one way to breakthrough.

The dispute over the occupation of the Sinai desert

by Israel became locked into inflexible positions: Israel would not withdraw and Egypt would not refrain from attacking Israel. By examining each party's interests – Israel in secure frontiers, Egypt in peaceful occupation of its own territory, the Sinai – the parties were eventually persuaded to trade land for security.

The negotiator-as-mediator can initiate exploration of each party's interests by the basic communication skills of the debate phase:

- Actively listening to the other negotiator and looking for expressions of interests (concerns, needs, fear, motives)
- Questioning to highlight interests
- Summarizing to clarify what lies behind specific wants
- Reframing the issues to reveal alternative solutions to interests

Interests and Options

The negotiator-as-mediator does not focus on the declared positions of the other negotiator. This is a cause of deadlock. Simply denying people what they want is a negative approach and it can be perceived as being threatening.

By shifting the emphasis on to why they want something (their interests) it might be possible to step sideways round the inflexible position and consider other options.

For example, a local community opposed to a runway extension wants the extension plans abandoned. The airway authorities want to proceed with them. A deadlock ensues. But what are the interests of the local community? Is it no runway (their want) or less noise (their interest)? Can something similar be achieved that does not preclude a runway extension but does preclude noisy jets flying in and out 24 hours a day?

Generating new options is a useful way to break through deadlock. If linked to perceptive assessments of their interests, progress can be made in finding a solution. Having identified an interest, the next important step is to engage with them in searching for other solutions.

It is important that we do not swap an obsession with 'sacred' positions for an obsession with the 'magic' of identifying interests. The connection between a party's interests and the negotiable issues developed to secure those interests, and the positions adopted to fix the details, is not one of 'interests good; issues and positions bad'.

Interests, issues and positions are inextricably linked. No one of the three dominates the other two. Use these concepts as tools to break through when deadlocked.

If the parties are deadlocked over a position on an issue, turn to interests to see if there are other options (i.e., other issues and positions) that can deliver the interests.

If the interests of the parties are diametrically opposed it serves no purpose to try to change either parties regard for their interests. That approach becomes a source of deeper conflict.

By turning from the confrontation of interests to the negotiation of the more mundane issues and their associated positions, we seek to find a way through the deadlock on the major themes of interest by making progress of the negotiable detail.

Interests cannot be negotiated – like principles they are above negotiation – but their application in each and every case can be negotiated. Negotiation is about detail, not about people having interests (their fears, hopes, and concerns). Detail is about the negotiable issues and the ranges of positions embedded in the issues.

The search for new options is a search for new issues and positions, uncontaminated by previous attitude sets and prejudices. An option, remember, is a negotiable remedy that delivers an interest, which is another name for a negotiable issue.

To assist this process the negotiator-as-mediator tries to set standards by which options will be discussed (better by example than initially by precept because the negotiator's motives may be challenged).

A common cause of failure in searching for new options is that of the negotiators making premature judgements about what is proposed or tentatively suggested. Brain-storming techniques are useful here. Separating the process of inventing new options from judging them helps otherwise fragile new ideas survive long enough to be seriously considered, which could mean that they themselves lead to other options which are more credible.

The negotiator strives constantly to challenge the view that the only solution possible is the impossible one that is driving the negotiators into deadlock. Retreating into defences based on denying that there is a problem with the single option on the table, or asserting that if there is a problem it is not one shared by you, is utterly counter-productive. If deadlock is a problem then the solution that is creating that deadlock is a problem too. A co-operative effort to create some new options is worthwhile for both negotiators.

Values
By putting yourself in their shoes, if only as a mind game – without adopting their positions, but trying to

see why they have adopted them – you will discover underlying value differences. Behind interests stand a person's values.

Values are the belief systems that give people their views of the world, how it works and their place in it. They are a long time in emerging and are usually very difficult to shift once they are entrenched. They can be implanted in childhood or by stressful adult experience (the 'Pauline conversion' for example, or the traumas of a recession, war, divorce or ecstatic experience). They are inculcated by a community – or lack of one – and by one's personal life history. They guide what the negotiator believes to be true.

For example, the vexed question of repatriated profits occasionally arises in international relations. The host country is desperately short of capital and wants foreign investment. It wants to hang on to every bit of the investment and sees profits as a drain on its (usually) scarce foreign currency holdings. Its values lead it to believe that foreign capitalists are plunderers of the nation's wealth. So it refuses repatriation.

But this conflicts with its interests – improving domestic added value from the wages of those employed in the investment – and with the interests of the foreign investor (seeking profits from its investment). Hence, foreign investment falls in this country and with it domestic added value. The foreign capitalist sees the potential host country as a greedy and corrupt regime out to exploit the gullible investor. They regard repatriation as the litmus test of the host country's intentions. A clash of wants (added value or profits) looms because values clash or are threatened.

In the clash of value the negotiator faces the most difficult of all deadlocks. Any attempts that are perceived to change somebody's values are bitterly resisted. If a dispute is raised into a struggle of values the spiral of conflict can slide rapidly into total opposition. This leads to clear advice: understand a negotiator's values, even study them, but make no moves to challenge them in any way.

This creates problems when we are not sure of the other negotiator's values. This is yet another recommendation for listening to what the other negotiator says, how they say it, the specific words used, the phrases and clichés scattered in their sentences and any stereotypes they let slip out. These will reflect their values.

Be wary of springing to the defence of your own values. It is better to acknowledge the clear differences in values in a non-threatening and non-condemnatory way. This is especially true when dealing across cultures in countries other than the one with which you are familiar. The more you know about the other negotiator's values in a deadlock situation, the more likely you are to avoid the sort of misunderstandings that lead to avoidable disputes.

When in a country where you are the foreigner it is best that you remember that your political views are only relevant where you vote, that your religion is between you and your maker, that your moral code is between you and your life partner, that your ethics are between you and your legal system and that what else goes on in that country is none of your business – *if* you want to do business there (and in some unhappy places wish to leave the country unmolested).

Emotions

Of course, emotional considerations are not avoidable. In disputes they arise inevitably from the commitment each negotiator has to their preferred solution. The question centres on how they should be handled.

Recognizing somebody's emotions is an obvious first step to accommodating to them in the sense that they have as much right to feel emotional about something as you do. Telling somebody that you feel something about an event (for instance, an apparent slur) might be enough to prevent its re-occurrence. True, they might take advantage of your revelation and mock you. This at least tells you what you are dealing with. But asserting the legitimacy of the other negotiator to have and express emotions in the negotiations might help build a bridge between you.

Negotiators sometimes express themselves abrasively because they feel intensely about something. They might also do this as part of their efforts to dominate you. But the advice given earlier applies. Because you are not going to be fazed in the slightest by dominating behaviour you are not going to react emotionally to their emotional outbursts. You need not retaliate with a display of your own. You understand that they have rights to be emotional without you having to agree that they are right to insist on their solution.

It always comes down to what you do next. If you are the cause of their emotional outburst, apologize for the unintended action (remember the merits of their case) and graciously accept their apologies if the situation is reversed.

CHECKLIST FOR DIFFICULT DISPUTES

- Adopt the negotiator-as-mediator role
- Search for their interests as the motivators of their wants
- Use debate techniques to uncover hidden interests
- Search for their values

- Do not challenge, criticize, or threaten the other negotiator's values
- Understand their values as the cause of their motivations (interests)
- Generate new options by refraining from premature judgement of proposed solutions
- Seek agreement on the substantive issues using new options to meet each party's interests

Common mistakes to avoid
- Ignoring the role of interests in generating wants
- Preferring the satisfaction of mutual failure to the successful conclusion of a dispute
- Attacking the other negotiator's values
- Instantly rejecting attempts to discover new options

A perfect negotiation?
Working as a temporary part-time barman in my brother-in-law's hotel in the west of Scotland, I noticed a local resident was buying customers in the public bar glasses of whisky.

On enquiring why the generosity, he replied that he had just sold his waterlogged boat in the loch for £6,000 and proclaimed proudly that he never expected anybody to buy it at a tenth of that price.

On finishing my shift I went through to the dining room to have dinner with my family. I noticed a young lady at a table with several companions and a couple of bottles of champagne. She was someone I had not seen since university.

On enquiring as to the cause of her champagne celebration she told me that she had just acquired a boat, which her carpenters and painters would work on tomorrow to make it look like a luxury cruiser for a film sequence her company was shooting.

She explained that she was the 'Props Manager' for the production team and had been given a budget of £16,000 to acquire a suitable boat, which was to be burnt after the scene was shot as part of the thriller they were filming.

As she had bought the old boat for £6,000 she was well within her budget and this would be of great satisfaction to her producer when he arrived the next day. Hence, her celebration. And, I could not help thinking, the genial satisfaction of the local ex-boat owner celebrating next door in the public bar!

When both parties to a negotiation have clear cause to be satisfied with the negotiated deal they strike, that is about as close as you can get to a 'perfect negotiation'.

PERFECT NEGOTIATOR'S COMPETENCE TEST

A short forced-choice competence test follows for you to test your understanding of the main concepts presented in the previous ten chapters.

Mark the answer, which in your opinion is the most appropriate answer from the ones provided.

1. **We should negotiate when:**
   a) it would be a sign of weakness to give in
   b) we need them more than they need us
   c) both parties can say 'no'
   d) when they need us more than we need them

2. **A negotiator's entry price is:**
   a) the price a negotiator prefers
   b) the price a negotiator must get
   c) the price the other negotiator might agree to
   d) the price the negotiator opens at

3. **Blue behaviour is characterised by:**
   a) being generous
   b) giving as much as you take
   c) being overly concerned with pleasing the other negotiator
   d) being assertive

4. **Negotiators prioritise:**
   a) negotiable issues
   b) entry and exit points
   c) ranges of positions
   d) proposals and bargains

5. **An interest is:**
   a) anything important to the negotiator

b) the motive for preferring some outcomes to others
c) something the negotiators have in common
d) a negotiator's hidden agenda

6. In the debate phase negotiators should:
   a) discover the other negotiator's wants
   b) complete it quickly to avoid arguments
   c) ensure the other negotiator understands your position
   d) refrain from disclosing your wants

7. Negotiators signal:
   a) that a proposal is imminent
   b) a desire for the listener to move
   c) a willingness to consider movement
   d) a preference for compromise

8. The most effective way to handle disagreement is to:
   a) point out where the other negotiator is wrong
   b) explain courteously the grounds for your disagreement
   c) summarize the case against the other negotiator's views
   d) ask questions

9. Red behaviour is characterised by:
   a) taking more than you give
   b) being openly aggressive and rude
   c) trying to humiliate the other negotiator
   d) intimidating the other negotiator

10. In the proposal phases the negotiator should:
    a) ask questions
    b) be non-specific in the condition and specific in

the offer

c) be specific in the condition and specific in the offer

d) be specific in the condition and non-specific in the offer

11. A tradable is:

a) anything you want to trade

b) anything on the agenda

c) anything you prefer

d) anything over which the negotiators have discretion and at least one of them values

12. A bargain is:

a) a specific condition and a non-specific offer

b) a specific condition and a specific offer

c) a non-specific condition and a specific offer

d) a good deal

13. Purple behaviour is characterized by:

a) alternating between red and blue behaviour

b) adding blue to red behaviour

c) linking red demands with blue offers

d) neutralizing red behaviour with blue offers

14. Effective negotiators:

a) prepare before they negotiate

b) behave appropriately in each of the Four Phases

c) bargain after they have proposed

d) signal before they propose

Suggested solutions:
1c; 2d; 3c; 4a; 5b; 6a; 7c; 8d; 9a; 10d; 11d; 12b; 13c; 14b

Comments on the suggested solutions should be sent to: <gavin@negweb.com>

PERFECT CAREER

Max Eggert

In a world where job opportunities are continually shrinking it is more important than ever before to actively manage your career. More time is spent at work than in any other activity, so it is vital to make sure that you are following the correct path.

The Perfect Career adjusts the balance in your favour, first by helping you to make a thorough analysis of your skills, experiences and values, and then providing practical strategies to enable you to achieve your career ambitions.

£6.99   1844131459

PERFECT CV

Max Eggert

Whether you're applying for your first job or planning an all-important career move, your CV is the most potent strike weapon in your armoury. This classic, bestselling book is a concise and invaluable guide that gives you the blueprint for the perfect CV. It shows you clearly and quickly how to present you and your skills and experience in the best possible way – and how to avoid the many easily-made mistakes which swiftly antagonize potential employers.

£6.99   1844131440

PERFECT INTERVIEW

Max Eggert

Perfect Interview is comprehensive, but concise and to-the-point. It shows you quickly and clearly how to present yourself and your skills in the best possible way at an interview. Packed with success, tips and checklists, it will enable you to make sure the interview goes the way *you* want it to – and that the result is a job offer that's satisfactory to both you and your new employer.

£6.99   1844131432

PERFECT PEOPLE SKILLS

Andrew Floyer Acland

Perfect People Skills helps you to deal with other people effectively and how to be aware of your own behaviour too. Differences of direction and motivation, personality, ethnic group, gender, class and ability can all bring problems, as well as those presented by 'difficult types'. The author provides some powerful ideas for preventing people problems, resolving conflict and building harmonious homes and workplaces.

The book is comprehensive and yet concise and to-the-point. It is written in simple, clear language and is designed to be of immediate, practical benefit to readers in developing better relationships at work and outside work.

Chapters include:

Grounding	Listening
Questioning	Empathising
Speaking	Negotiating
Proposing	Counselling
Confronting	Preventing

**Order further Arrow titles
from your local bookshop, or have them delivered
direct to your door by Bookpost**

---

arrow books